EXERCISES IN FRENCH PHONICS

FRANCIS W. NACHTMANN
University of Illinois at Urbana - Champaign

ISBN 978-0-87563-215-5

Published By

STIPES PUBLISHING L.L.C.
204 West University Avenue
Champaign, Illinois 61820

TABLE OF CONTENTS

PREFACE

These exercises are intended to give practice in matching the correct sounds to the French spellings. They may be used at any level from the first year of high school French to the third or fourth year of college French—wherever the student betrays a weakness in the skills which these exercises are intended to correct. Once a student has passed the elementary stage of learning French, he acquires the majority of his new words through the printed form. He must know what sounds the spellings represent and be put on guard against attributing English values to the French spellings. The teacher needs additional examples to reinforce his classroom corrections; these exercises should fill that need.

It is assumed that the student has had some practice in making the basic sounds. They are not described in detail here, and improvement in the quality of sound production or of intonation will have to be based on imitation of live or recorded models. This text and its exercises are limited to pronunciation problems originating with the spelling. For example, whereas only the teacher can train his students in the proper dentalization of the French *t*, the exercises dealing with the *t* in this manual are designed to accustom the student to pronouncing the *th* as a [t] when he sees it, or to remind him that the *t* in certain spellings is pronounced [s], or that the *d* in liaison is linked as a *t*.

The various orthographical problems cannot be entirely separated from one another; occasionally words used in one exercise exemplify several difficulties and anticipate some that are to be covered in a later section. But it is expected that the student will not be limited to going through the text merely once, rather that he will review it as often as is necessary to give him assurance on all the points treated.

The phenomena of spelling and pronunciation are not treated as dry, isolated facts. Allusions to analogous English usages, to historical explanations, and to sources of interference between the languages are introduced to increase the student's linguistic background, and particularly in order to make a point of French pronunciation easier for him to acquire. An apparent idiosyncrasy of French spelling or pronunciation should seem much simpler to the learner if he can be shown that it already exists in English, or if the precise reason for his problem in French can be pinpointed at its source in his own language.

The exercises usually contain words, sometimes phrases, occasionally artificial sentences composed to bring together words of a similar type of pronunciation challenge. No connected texts are provided because they can be found in the nearest French book.

Often the vocabulary of the exercises will go beyond what the student presently knows. This is intentional. The purpose is to accustom him to pronouncing correctly any French word he encounters, as long as it conforms to the usual rules. Occasional translations are provided when it is thought that the meanings will aid the student in remembering an exception or a special example.

The *International Phonetic Alphabet* is used where necessary to clarify or reinforce a point, and a *Key to the Phonetic Symbols* is found in the appendix. The length sign for vowels in the phonetic transcriptions is omitted as irrelevant to our present purpose, and phonetic symbols are used sparingly since it is the aim of this manual to encourage the student to pronounce well directly from the spelling.

Not all the possible pronunciation problems are taken up, but the experienced teacher will recognize that the majority of the perennial trouble spots are covered. If the average student could acquire assurance on just the matters treated here, there would be a great reduction in the ranks of those who say apologetically, "You'll have to excuse my pronunciation. I've only had two years of French."

SUGGESTIONS FOR USE

The material in this manual can be covered in small installments of five to ten minutes' time worked into the class period along with the regular assignments. The manual need not be used every day, but reasonably regular practice with it should be continued until its material is covered. Even then it should not be dropped, but should be reviewed regularly whenever class errors on a particular point indicate that some section should be restudied. A review every semester or every year of the points treated here is desirable, even necessary, as a teacher inherits a new class or receives transfer students from other schools or teachers.

The shorter sections in the manual can form an adequate assignment for one day's drill. Occasionally, the teacher might assign two short sections for a single day. In the longer sections the teacher should assign only a part for a single day's recitation; for example, Chapter VI on *The Nasal Vowels* would take at least four days to cover. The assignment should always be kept short, never to exceed ten minutes of drill.

To have each student in turn pronounce a single word in class recitations of the exercises would usually result in too piecemeal a performance. A better arrangement is to have the first student pronounce items 1–5, the next student take the following five, and so forth. Or the instructor can interrupt at irregular intervals to have another student continue, letting each one pronounce from three to ten items. The exercise can be repeated from the beginning until everyone has had a chance to recite. If a reciter makes an error on a point other than the one currently being studied, he should be corrected quickly and with a minimum of digression, unless the error involves a point previously studied. A variant of the recitation technique, which keeps the whole class participating, is to have the class chorus each pronunciation after the solo reciter.

The teacher may want to give a brief introduction to a new pronunciation lesson before launching his students on it, or he may simply assign it directly for study, depending on his estimate of his class. Once a point has been studied, the teacher should insist absolutely that it be applied in all subsequent class work. He should avoid merely making a hasty correction and restating the rule when a reciting student makes an error. Rather, he should halt the offender and invite him or his classmates to point out the error, correct it, and, if appropriate, formulate the rule covering it. Every effort should be made to shift to the student the responsibility for learning, retaining, and applying these phonic principles.

CHAPTER I

FINAL CONSONANTS

1

Final consonants in French are generally silent, with the exception of **c, r, f,** and **l,** all exemplified in the word CaReFuL.[1] This rule is already obvious in the host of English borrowings from French, in which English *usually* retains the French treatment of the final consonant. For example, pronounce the following "English" words:

ballet	crochet	bric-a-brac
bouquet	debris	Cadillac
buffet	debut	chic
Chevrolet	depot	amateur
corps	filet	chauffeur
coup	richochet	chef

EXERCISES

A. Pronounce the following French words, all of which have a silent final consonant.

1. l'acha~~t~~
2. anglai~~s~~
3. aprè~~s~~
4. autrefoi~~s~~
5. l'avoca~~t~~
6. le bouque~~t~~
7. le cabare~~t~~
8. chau~~d~~
9. la Chevrole~~t~~
10. che~~z~~
11. le dépô~~t~~
12. Détroi~~t~~
13. le do~~s~~
14. écri~~t~~
15. étroi~~t~~
16. exqui~~s~~
17. la forê~~t~~
18. le galo~~p~~
19. l'intérê~~t~~
20. intéressan~~t~~
21. jalou~~x~~
22. le moi~~s~~
23. parfai~~t~~
24. le pay~~s~~
25. préci~~s~~
26. le pri~~x~~
27. le proje~~t~~
28. les propo~~s~~
29. pui~~s~~
30. surpri~~s~~

[1] Proper nouns do not necessarily conform to the usual rules of pronunciation, and family names may be pronounced in any way the owner wishes. If the proper noun is French and has the usual combinations of letters that one sees in modern French, the chances are that it is pronounced regularly. If it is a foreign name or has some unexpected combination of letters, it should be checked with an authoritative source.

B. Pronounce the following words, all of which end in a pronounced **c, r, f,** or **l.**

1. avec
2. le bac
3. le bric-à-brac
4. Cadillac
5. chic
6. le duc
7. sec
8. agir
9. l'air
10. l'amour
11. car
12. le créateur
13. finir
14. sur
15. fier (*adj.*)
16. actif
17. le bœuf
18. bref
19. le chef
20. l'œuf
21. le tarif
22. vif
23. l'appel
24. le fil
25. l'hôtel
26. idéal
27. il
28. le matériel
29. mondial
30. professionnel

1.1 The rule summarized in CaReFuL can also be applied to words of the following type, in which the **r** represents the final sound.

1. d'abor~~d~~
2. l'accor~~d~~
3. lour~~d~~
4. le retar~~d~~
5. tar~~d~~
6. alor~~s~~
7. diver~~s~~
8. enver~~s~~
9. l'univer~~s~~
10. le cor~~ps~~
11. couver~~t~~
12. le dépar~~t~~
13. l'effor~~t~~
14. le rappor~~t~~
15. le spor~~t~~
16. le tor~~t~~

---

2 EXCEPTIONS

The key word CaReFuL as a guide to pronounced final consonants is, after all, only a rule of thumb, and there are exceptions. Some exceptions can be treated as groups; others have to be learned individually.

2.1 The **r** is silent in the ending **-er** of first-conjugation infinitives and in most nouns and adjectives of two or more syllables. Pronounce the following examples.

1. ajouter
2. attirer
3. donner
4. fonder
5. prier
6. l'escalier
7. le millier
8. le papier
9. le soulier
10. le chantier
11. premier
12. entier
13. dernier
14. léger
15. particulier

But: la cuiller [kɥijɛr] *spoon*
also spelled cuillère

2.2 The **c** is usually silent in the ending **-nc.**

1. le ban~~c~~ *bench*
2. blan~~c~~ *white*
3. le flan~~c~~ *flank, side*
4. fran~~c~~ *frank*
5. le jon~~c~~ *reed*
6. le tron~~c~~ *trunk*
7. il vain~~c~~ *he conquers*

But: donc [dɔ̃k] *therefore, so* (except when used as an intensifier: Dis donc [dɔ̃])

2.3 The relationship of spelling to pronunciation is erratic in words ending in **-ct** and **-pt.**

Final **-ct, -pt** *silent:*		*Final* **-ct, -pt** *pronounced:*
	-act	
exa~~ct~~ [ɛgza] *or* [ɛgzakt]		le tact le contact l'impact
	-ect	
l'aspe~~ct~~ le respe~~ct~~ suspe~~ct~~		abject direct indirect infect *foul*
	-nct	
distin~~ct~~ [distɛ̃] l'instin~~ct~~ [ɛ̃stɛ̃]		
	-pt	
prom~~pt~~ [prɔ̃]		abrupt le concept le rapt *abduction* le script

2.4 The following common words are individual exceptions to the rule about final consonants. They are words in which a final **c, r, f,** or **l** is silent, or in which other final consonants are pronounced.

Final consonants pronounced:

1. est [ɛst] *east*
2. ouest [wɛst] *west*
3. sud [syd] *south*
   But: nord [nɔr] *north*

4. l'as [as] *ace*
5. l'autobus [ɔ(o)tɔbys] *bus*
6. l'omnibus [ɔmnibys] *local train*
7. le bifteck [biftɛk] *beefsteak*
8. le cap [kap] *cape*
9. le coq [kɔk] *cock, rooster*
10. la dot [dɔt] *dowry*
11. le fils [fis] *son*
12. le gaz [gɑz] *gas*
13. hélas [elɑs] *alas*
14. l'index [ɛ̃dɛks] *index*
15. le maïs [mais] *corn*
16. les mœurs [mœrs] *customs, mores*
17. net [nɛt] *clear, neat*
18. le sens [sɑ̃s] *sense, meaning; direction*
19. le tennis [tɛnis] *tennis*
20. le vasistas [vazistɑs] *transom*

Final consonants silent:

1. l'estomac [ɛstɔma] *stomach*
2. le tabac [taba] *tobacco*
3. le porc [pɔr] *pig, pork*
4. la clef [kle] *key*
   alternate spelling: la clé
5. le fusil [fyzi] *gun*
6. gentil [ʒɑ̃ti] *nice*
7. l'outil [uti] *tool*
8. le sourcil [sursi] *eyebrow*

There are other exceptions to the rule about pronunciation of final consonants, but they are less common. Memorize the above list as a very serviceable beginning. Others can be learned with increasing exposure to French.

REVIEW EXERCISES

These exercises contain words exemplifying the observations of the preceding paragraphs about silent and pronounced final consonants.

A. Pronounce the following words.

1. aimer
2. amateur
3. l'appétit
4. l'arrêt
5. l'assaut
6. aussitôt

7. bas
8. beaucoup
9. le bœuf
10. le bourg
11. le canif
12. chanter
13. le chanteur
14. le chantier
15. chic
16. le ciel
17. le conférencier
18. le concours
19. le couvert
20. la cuiller
21. les débris
22. le début
23. égal
24. extérieur
25. l'hiver
26. industriel
27. le lac
28. local
29. le loup
30. mais
31. Marc
32. la mer
33. mobiliser
34. le mobilier
35. naturel
36. le nœud
37. le parc
38. la part
39. planer
40. planter
41. le planteur
42. le porc
43. porter
44. le porteur
45. poser
46. le poseur
47. public
48. rétroactif
49. le sac
50. la soif
51. suppressif
52. le suif
53. le tic
54. le trésor
55. le vernis
56. la voix

B. Continue as in the preceding exercise.

1. les troncs légers
2. les derniers joncs
3. un Grec franc
4. un romancier discret
5. un index exact
6. un contact suspect
7. les joncs près des troncs
8. l'objet direct et l'objet indirect
9. des sourcils distincts
10. un concept tout particulier de l'instinct
11. Il est trop fier pour se fier à nous.
12. Le montagnard montrait un mépris des mœurs.
13. Les loups rôdaient sur les débris.
14. Il sentait l'odeur du sol autour du bourg.
15. En suivant son instinct le sujet s'approchait du pied du mur extérieur près duquel poussait du maïs, mais il ne voyait pas les chats.
16. L'impact du coup sur le sol blanc fut le seul effet distinct noté.
17. Hélas, le fils avait un as.
18. La côte est, étroite et abrupte, est humide et boisée. La côte ouest est beaucoup plus étalée.

Note: The exceptions are worked into the exercise above at a much higher frequency than they would occur in a French text. But if the exceptions can be remembered, the reader can depend on the CaReFuL rule as a guide to pronunciation of the vast majority of other final consonants.

---

3 ADDITIONAL SPECIAL EXCEPTIONS

There are certain words whose final consonant is silent in some uses, but pronounced in others.

3.1 The final consonant of the following nouns is pronounced in the singular, but silent in the plural.

Singular	*Plural*	
l'œuf	les œuf̸s̸	[lezø]
le bœuf	les bœuf̸s̸	[lebø]
l'os	les os̸	[lezo]

3.2 **Plus:** The final consonant (except in liaison) is silent:
(a) When **plus** is used before an adjective or an adverb (***plus*** *grand,* ***plus*** *vite*);
(b) When used as an adverb of quantity (*Il faut* ***plus*** *de patience.*);
(c) When used as a negative (*Il* ***ne*** *vient* ***plus*** *nous voir. Paul n'étudie pas* ***non plus.***).

Otherwise it is generally pronounced [plys]:
(a) When it is the final word in an adverbial phrase (*au* ***plus,*** *tout au* ***plus,*** *de* ***plus***);
(b) In the mathematical meaning "plus" (*Trois* ***plus*** *deux font cinq.*).

3.3 **Tous:** The final consonant is silent when **tous** is an adjective (***tous*** *les garcons,* ***tous*** *mes amis,* ***tous*** *ceux, etc.*), but pronounced when **tous** is a pronoun (*Ils viennent* ***tous.***).

3.4 **Soit:** The final consonant is regularly silent in all uses except in the meaning ***Soit!*** *Agreed! So be it!*

3.5 **Chef-d'œuvre** [ʃedœvr]: The **f** is silent in this compound word, although it is regularly pronounced in all other uses of **chef.**

3.6 **Le Christ** [krist]: Final consonants pronounced.
Jésu~~s~~-Chri~~st~~ [ʒezykri]: Final consonants silent.

3.7 The numerals, which vary considerably according to position, are treated separately. (See Chapter XXII.)

4

Verb endings obey the rule that final consonants are silent, but in addition, the entire endings **-es** and **-ent** are silent wherever they occur. The following paradigms give a sampling of tenses, particularly those with silent **-es** in certain forms.

Present	*Present*	*Past Definite*
je retourn~~e~~	je ven~~ds~~	je parlai
tu retourn~~es~~	tu ven~~ds~~	tu parla~~s~~
il retourn~~e~~	il ven~~d~~	il parla
nous retournon~~s~~	nous vendon~~s~~	nous parlâm~~es~~
vous retourne~~z~~	vous vende~~z~~	vous parlât~~es~~
ils retourn~~ent~~	ils vend~~ent~~	ils parlèr~~ent~~

Past Definite	*Past Definite*	
je lu~~s~~	je vin~~s~~	[vɛ̃]
tu lu~~s~~	tu vin~~s~~	[vɛ̃]
il lu~~t~~	il vin~~t~~	[vɛ̃]
nous lûm~~es~~	nous vînm~~es~~	[vɛ̃m]
vous lût~~es~~	vous vînt~~es~~	[vɛ̃t]
ils lur~~ent~~	ils vinr~~ent~~	[vɛ̃r]

EXERCISE

This exercise offers practice in pronouncing verb forms which end in a silent **-es** or **-ent.**

1. ils utilisent
2. ils tirent
3. ils jettent
4. ils envoient

5. ils ralentissent
6. ils surprennent
7. tu triomphes
8. ils gardent
9. tu gardes
10. ils tendaient
11. ils lisaient
12. que tu suives
13. ils faufilaient
14. ils approchèrent
15. ils firent
16. ils connurent
17. ils envoyèrent
18. elles tirèrent
19. ils discernèrent
20. ils pendirent
21. ils comprirent
22. ils avaient
23. ils poussaient
24. elles auraient
25. ils seraient
26. elles virent
27. nous bouchâmes
28. vous remuâtes
29. nous jetâmes
30. vous jetâtes
31. vous tirâtes
32. nous voulûmes
33. vous voulûtes
34. nous finîmes
35. vous sortîtes
36. ils purent
37. ils durent
38. ils durèrent
39. que tu susses
40. qu'ils rompissent
41. nous rendîmes
42. vous expliquâtes
43. nous reçûmes
44. vous revîtes
45. elles s'enrichirent

4.1 The silent **-ent** ending of the third person plural is found in all tenses of the indicative and subjunctive except the future. Pronounce the following verb forms.

Present	*Imperfect*	*Past Definite*
ils donn~~ent~~	ils donnai~~ent~~	ils donnèr~~ent~~
ils rend~~ent~~	ils rendai~~ent~~	ils rendir~~ent~~
ils reçoiv~~ent~~	ils recevai~~ent~~	ils reçur~~ent~~

Future	*Conditional*
ils donneron~~t~~	ils donnerai~~ent~~
ils rendron~~t~~	ils rendrai~~ent~~
ils recevron~~t~~	ils recevrai~~ent~~

Pres. Subjunctive	*Imperf. Subjunctive*
ils donn~~ent~~	ils donnass~~ent~~
ils rend~~ent~~	ils rendiss~~ent~~
ils reçoiv~~ent~~	ils reçuss~~ent~~

REVIEW EXERCISE

This exercise is a review of all the paragraphs of this section.

1. La dot que les parents avaient donnée à la fille était d'un millier de francs.
2. Son unique outil et son seul péril étaient son fusil.
3. La jeune fille avait les cils blonds et les sourcils noirs.
4. Ils manquent de tact.
5. Ils conservèrent les œufs dans ce local.
6. Ils lavent les cuillers comme par instinct avant de s'en servir.
7. Nous partîmes au galop pour le cap en prenant le chemin direct.
8. Ils jouaient aux échecs.
9. Le retour des bœufs à l'étable fut prompt.
10. Un concept exact n'est jamais suspect.
11. Tous les inspecteurs visitèrent la ferme mais tous ne furent pas contents de leur visite.
12. Le tabac lui donnait mal à l'estomac.
13. Le sol ici est plus compact.
14. Tous les œufs étaient intacts.
15. Les bœufs regardaient tous vers l'ouest.
16. Ils sont montés jusqu'au sommet du pic.
17. Le chef du musée leur montrait des chefs-d'œuvre.
18. Mais le maïs n'est pas un produit de l'est.
19. Ces propositions comprennent un objet direct et un objet indirect.
20. Nous vendîmes tous les couteaux et toutes les cuillers.
21. Ils seront les premiers et aussi les derniers à visiter le chantier.
22. Tu cherches un index exact?
23. Les industriels témoignèrent d'un profond respect des mœurs.
24. Nous naissons tous fous.
25. Les draps sont trop courts pour les matelas dans le cabinet.

CHAPTER II

INTERVOCALIC S

5

S between vowels in French is always given the voiced sound—that is, it is pronounced [z]. What causes English speakers to mispronounce it in French is that the English **intervocalic s** is voiced in some words, unvoiced in others. You will note this variance in the following English words.

Voiced	*Unvoiced*
1. nose	dose
2. phrase	base
3. pose	verbose
4. tease	obese
5. use (*verb*)	use (*noun*)
6. close (*verb*)	close (*adjective*)

EXERCISES

A. Pronounce the French words listed below, taking care that each **s** between vowels is pronounced [z].

1. la rose
2. la dose
3. la phrase
4. la bise
5. la fraise
6. qu'il lise
7. il vise
8. usager
9. il abuse
10. le philosophe
11. qu'il conduise
12. le réseau
13. la philosophie
14. l'hypocrisie
15. obèse
16. on basait
17. nous baserons
18. la besace
19. mesurer
20. le visage
21. la valise
22. il grise
23. qu'il dise
24. l'asile
25. la mésaventure
26. la maison

27. la saison	39. l'oiseau
28. la curiosité	40. usurper
29. le diocèse	41. la poésie
30. l'hérésie	42. décisif
31. la raison	43. l'artisan
32. il disait	44. la prosodie
33. résigner	45. l'excuse
34. résolu	46. la bêtise
35. disant	47. suffisant
36. oisif	48. le besoin
37. l'extase	49. voisine
38. l'épisode	50. isolé

B. The importance of pronouncing the **intervocalic s** correctly can be seen in the following pairs of words. Mispronunciation of the word in the first column by failure to voice the **s** would cause the word to be understood as given in the second column.

1. il lise *from* lire	il lisse *from* lisser
2. baiser *kiss*	baisser *to lower*
3. viser *to aim*	visser *to screw*
4. il vise	il visse
5. base *base*	basse *low*
6. vous présentez *you present*	vous pressentez *you have a presentiment*
7. une ruse *a ruse*	une Russe *a Russian woman*
8. embraser *to set fire to*	embrasser *to kiss, embrace*
9. casé *filed*	cassé *broken*
10. le cousin *cousin*	le coussin *cushion*
11. le désert *desert*	le dessert *dessert*
12. le poison *poison*	le poisson *fish*
13. croisant *crossing, passing*	croissant *crescent*
14. ce rasoir *this razor*	se rasseoir *to sit down again*
15. il l'épouse *he marries her*	il les pousse *he pushes them*

CHAPTER III

WORDS ENDING IN MUTE E

6

A **mute e** at the end of a French word indicates that the preceding consonant is pronounced. A preceding vowel is, of course, also pronounced. An **e** at the end of a word is always mute unless it bears an acute accent.

EXERCISES

A. Pronounce the following words, sounding all the letters up to the **mute e.**

1. achète̸
2. jalouse̸
3. anime̸
4. donne̸
5. sale̸
6. pose̸
7. compresse̸
8. libère̸
9. sonate̸
10. commode̸
11. remette̸
12. lise̸
13. élabore̸
14. couverte̸
15. précise̸
16. brève̸
17. Molière̸
18. avoue̸
19. finie̸
20. effraie̸

B. Practice the following columns, noting the effect of the **e** in the second spelling of each pair.

1. mis̸
mise̸ [miz]
2. parfait̸
parfaite̸
3. exquis̸
exquise̸
4. chaud̸
chaude̸
5. complet̸
complète̸
6. couvert̸
couverte̸
7. divers̸
diverse̸
8. dit̸
dite̸
9. dernier̸* [dɛrnje]
dernière̸ [dɛrnjɛr]
10. léger̸* [leʒe]
légère̸ [leʒɛr]
11. rapport̸
rapporte̸
12. clos̸
close̸
13. promp̸t̸ [prɔ̃]
promp̸te̸ [prɔ̃t]
14. distinc̸t̸ [distɛ̃]
distincte̸ [distɛ̃kt]

15. do~~s~~
    dos~~e~~ [doz]
16. tan~~t~~
    tant~~e~~
17. chan~~t~~
    chant~~e~~
18. sen~~t~~
    sent~~e~~
19. fon~~t~~
    font~~e~~
20. respe~~ct~~
    respect~~e~~
21. suspe~~ct~~
    suspect~~e~~
22. galo~~p~~* [galo]
    galop~~e~~ [galɔp]
23. suje~~t~~
    sujett~~e~~
24. premie~~r~~* [prəmje]
    premièr~~e~~ [prəmjɛr]

*In certain words the vowel sound of the final syllable changes from [e] to [ɛ] or from [o] to [ɔ] with the addition of a final consonant sound. This is indicated in some cases by the addition of a grave accent, and is pointed out by the phonetic transcriptions in the dictionaries. A similar change also occurs in the pronunciation of most Frenchmen in pairs such as Numbers 5, 20, 21, 23, although the dictionaries do not acknowledge it.

C. Continue as in the preceding exercise.

1. frit
   frite
2. boulanger
   boulangère
3. épicier
   épicière
4. jet
   jette
5. bat
   batte
6. permis
   permise
7. accord
   accorde
8. bas
   base
9. idiot
   idiote
10. arrêt
    arrête
11. coût
    coûte
12. part
    parte
13. discret
    discrète
14. particulier
    particulière
15. chat
    chatte
16. flot
    flotte
17. éclat
    éclate
18. français
    française
19. anglais
    anglaise
20. marquis
    marquise
21. récit
    récite
22. surpris
    surprise
23. purifie [pyrifi]
    purifié [pyrifje]
24. fie [fi]
    fié [fje]
25. remercie
    remercié
26. marie
    marié
27. parie
    parié
28. certifie
    certifié
29. codifie
    codifié
30. rallie
    rallié

D. This exercise is intended to give additional practice in making instantaneous oral adjustment to various endings.

1. pris
   prise
   prisé
   prisée
2. content
   contente
   contenté
   contentée
3. complet
   complète
   complété
   complétée
4. bas
   base
   basse
   basé
   basée
5. vers
   verse
   versé
   versée
6. acquit [aki]
   acquitte
   acquitté
   acquittée
7. coup
   coupe
   coupé
   coupée
8. lis
   lise
   lisse
   lissé
   lissée
9. support
   supporte
   supporté
   supportée
10. souffert
    soufferte
11. souhait
    souhaite
    souhaité
12. brise
    brisé
13. fil
    file
    filé
14. cercle
    cerclé
15. coule
    coulé
16. compris
    comprise
17. touche
    touché
18. mérite
    mérité
19. mesure
    mesuré
20. isole
    isolé
21. exerce
    exercé
22. évite
    évité
23. frais
    fraise
24. chauffe
    chauffé
25. cite
    cité

CHAPTER IV

E Caduc

7

The **e caduc** means the falling or dropped **e.** It is so called because it usually becomes mute at the end of words and has a tendency to become mute elsewhere. When pronounced, it has the neutral sound [ə].

In English the sound [ə] can be represented in spelling by any vowel.

Pronounce the following English words, noting that the unstressed syllables all contain the vowel [ə] regardless of the spelling.

vital	opposite	foreign	elevate	consonant	ballot	coveted
[ə]	[ə][ə]	[ə]	[ə]	[ə][ə]	[ə]	[ə][ə]

In French, on the other hand, the sound [ə] is represented by the spelling **e** (with one exception; see Chapter VII, Paragraph 23.1) and regularly only in the following combinations:

(a) In the monosyllables **je, me, te, le, se, que, ce, de, ne.** (This is the complete list.)

(b) When **e** in the body of the word is followed
  (1) By a single consonant;
  (2) By a **consonant** + **l** or **r.**

Examples: (1) **le**vons, **re**venir, **re**latif, **re**çu, **me**sure, **re**pose, **re**tourne, **se**rai, **se**cours, **pe**sons

(2) **se**cret, **re**flet, **re**gret

EXERCISE

Pronounce the following words, all of which have one or more syllables containing the sound [ə].

1. devoir
2. geler
3. cheval
4. chevalier
5. chenal
6. gelé
7. orangerie
8. serons
9. peler
10. peser
11. donnerai
12. parlerons
13. retournerez
14. changerez
15. tirerai
16. rappelé
17. appliquerons
18. semer
19. velours
20. dedans
21. mener
22. repli
23. recevoir
24. redevable
25. chevelure
26. renouveler
27. regrette
28. menace
29. retrancher
30. retraite
31. reflet
32. relire
33. grommeler
34. reprise
35. Chevrolet
36. recevrai
37. revenue
38. redevenu
39. recommander
40. secret
41. secrétaire
42. représentatif
43. refuge
44. cheminée
45. relatif

8

In contrast to the above, **e** followed by doubled consonants (*se**rr**ai*, *ce**ss**ons*) or by any combination of two or more consonants (*pe**rt**e*, *me**rcr**edi*, *re**sp**e**ct**er*) has the open sound represented by the phonetic symbol [ɛ].

EXERCISE

In this exercise, make the contrast between words spelled with **e + one consonant** and those spelled with **e + two consonants.**

Note: e + two consonants = è = ê. All represent the sound [ɛ].

1. je serai *I shall be*
   je serrai *I tightened*
2. tu seras
   tu serras
3. il sera
   il serra
4. nous serons *we shall be*
   nous serrons *we tighten*

5. vous serez
   vous serrez
6. tu serais *you would be*
   tu serrais *you were tightening*
7. il serait
   il serrait
8. nous serions
   nous serrions
9. ils seraient
   ils serraient
10. la mesure
    le message
11. peser
    pessimisme
    pèse
    peste
12. reçu
    déçu
13. recevoir
    décevoir
14. nous pesons
    nous cessons
15. je ferai *I shall make*
    je ferrai *I shod (a horse)*
16. René
    renne
    rêne
    renier
    règne
17. selon
    selle
18. je jetai
    je jetterai
19. appeler
    appelle
20. nous appelons
    nous appellerons
21. Rabelais
    rebelle
22. la leçon
    la lessive

Note: The [ə] is essential to the meaning in many of these words. For example, *serai*, if mispronounced with an **open e,** could be interpreted as *serrai; leçon* as *laissons*, etc.

(In Numbers 12 and 13 above the contrast is between **e + a single consonant** and **é + a single consonant.**)

9 EXCEPTIONS

The two spellings **ress-** and **dess-** are exceptional in that the **e** is pronounced [ə] even before a double consonant. (Examples: *dessous, ressembler.*) This type of word is a compound consisting of the prefix **re** or **de + a word beginning with s:**

re + sembler = ressembler
re + sortir = ressortir
de + sous = dessous

In order to retain the **unvoiced s** [s] at the beginning of the original word, the **s** is doubled in the spelling. A single **s** at this juncture would normally indicate the sound [z] in French. (See Chapter II.)

EXERCISE

Pronounce the following words, which illustrate the sound [ə] spelled **e + ss.**

1. ressembler
2. le ressort
3. ressaisir
4. le ressentiment
5. ressentir
6. ressouvenir
7. la ressource
8. ressouder
9. dessus
10. au-dessus
11. le pardessus
12. dessous
13. au-dessous
14. le ressaut
15. resserrer

Note: Almost all the words beginning **ress-** have the vowel [ə] in the first syllable, but of the numerous words beginning **dess-** only ***dessus, dessous*** and their compounds take this sound.

10

The **e caduc** is dropped in the pronunciation of many of the words listed in this section. The same linguistic tendency which causes the English words *every* and *memory* to be reduced to two syllables (*ev'ry, mem'ry*) causes French words like ***donnerai, acheter, revenu,*** to be pronounced ***donn'rai, ach'ter, rev'nu.*** When there are two of these sounds in succession, as in **revenir,** or even a whole series, as in ***que je te le redemande,*** the French speaker suppresses approximately every other one. This habit takes much careful listening and imitation to reproduce accurately. It is not described here because it cannot be reduced to simple rules, and failure to achieve it is not disruptive of meaning as is the substitution of an incorrect sound for the [ə]. **Mute e**'s are still retained in singing and occasionally for emphasis or other reasons—not to mention certain regional dialects in which they are fully in evidence. For a natural, cultivated accent in French they must of course be suppressed as they are by speakers of standard French.

11

In summary, the spelling **e** represents the [ə] sound:

(a) In the list of monosyllables given;
(b) When it is followed by a single consonant (other than final);
(c) When it is followed by a **consonant + l** or **r;**
(d) In words beginning **ress-;**
(e) In ***dessous*** and ***dessus.***

REVIEW EXERCISE

In pronouncing the following words and phrases, give special attention to the combination of consonant sounds that follow the **e.** The exercise includes **e**'s pronounced [e], [ɛ], and [ə]. It does not include any **e**'s to be nasalized.

1. renier
2. mener
3. la meringue
4. venir
5. devenir
6. redevenir
7. les reliques
8. il le retourne
9. le secours
10. recevoir
11. décevoir
12. il repose
13. nous levons
14. dedans
15. dessus
16. dessous
17. il le dessine
18. la destinée
19. le désordre
20. achever
21. refléter
22. le secrétaire
23. repris
24. regreffer
25. régressif
26. au-dessous
27. le pardessus
28. qu'il vienne
29. la pelote
30. le pesage
31. le refuge
32. refermer
33. référer
34. ressouder
35. la résolution
36. repousser
37. la querelle
38. le ressort
39. petit
40. demeurer
41. chanceler
42. la requête
43. la cerise
44. la messe
45. la mesure
46. replier
47. la menace
48. nous serions
49. nous serrions
50. geler
51. la gélatine
52. vous levez
53. le levraut
54. la levrette
55. la lessive
56. le chevalier
57. il décevait
58. il recevait
59. vous semiez
60. le secret
61. vous feriez
62. le menuisier
63. que je regrette

64. Je venais de parler.
65. Il se le reprochait.
66. le menu
67. le mercenaire
68. la recherche
69. demi
70. demain
71. le grenier
72. regarder
73. le télescope
74. la muselière
75. l'atelier

CHAPTER V

SPECIAL PRONUNCIATIONS OF -IL, -ILL-, -ILLE

12

The spellings **-il** or **-ille** at the end of a word, or **-ill-** in the middle of a word, are pronounced [j] or [ij]. They do not represent the sound [l] except in **mille—ville—tranquille** and their derivatives. (Use as a memory device the phrase *mille villes tranquilles.*) Only one proper noun of frequency is pronounced with an [l]: *Lille.*

EXERCISES

A. Pronounce the following, which all contain the sound [l].

1. mille
   million
   milliard
   millier
   etc.
2. ville
   village
   Deauville
   etc.
3. tranquille
   tranquilliser
   tranquillité
   etc.

B. Pronounce the following, none of which contains the sound [l].

1. fille [fij]
2. famille [famij]
3. cheville [ʃəvij]
4. cédille [sedij]
5. quille [kij]
6. chenille [ʃənij]
7. pille [pij]
8. piller [pije]

9.	habillez	[abije]	25.	feuille	[fœj]
10.	sillon	[sijɔ̃]	26.	mouille	[muj]
11.	rail	[raj]	27.	mouillé	[muje]
12.	raille	[raj]	28.	grenouille	[grənuj]
13.	détail	[detaj]	29.	Anouilh	[anuj]
14.	détaille	[detaj]	30.	souille	[suj]
15.	pareil	[parɛj]	31.	bouillon	[bujɔ̃]
16.	pareille	[parɛj]	32.	infaillible	[ɛ̃fajibl]
17.	vieil	[vjɛj]	33.	veuillez	[vœje]
18.	vieille	[vjɛj]	34.	Noailles	[nɔaj]
19.	appareil	[aparɛj]	35.	jaillissant	[ʒajisɑ̃]
20.	bouteille	[butɛj]	36.	faillir	[fajir]
21.	œil	[œj]	37.	Chantilly	[ʃɑ̃tiji]
22.	deuil	[dœj]	38.	Chillon	[ʃijɔ̃]
23.	fauteuil	[fotœj]	39.	oreille	[ɔrɛj]
24.	veuille	[vœj]	40.	volaille	[vɔlaj]

Note: In Numbers 1–10 above the **-ill-** or **-ille** is pronounced [ij] when the **i** is the only vowel in the syllable. When another vowel precedes, the **-il, -ill-, -ille** is simply pronounced [j]: *rail, paillasse, mouille.*

It should be pointed out, although both French and English have the sound [j], only French can have it occurring at the end of a word, where the spellings **-il, -ille** are used to indicate it.

13

Words of the following type should not be confused with the spellings listed above. The words given below all contain the sound [l]. Observe how their spellings differ from those above.

1. la vallée
2. valider
3. nous allions
4. vous alliez
5. nous valions
6. vous valiez
7. calleux
8. le calligraphe
9. l'aile [ɛl]
10. l'aileron [ɛlrɔ̃]

With reference to Numbers 9 and 10, note that **-il** indicates the sound [j] only when it is final in the word and follows a vowel:

rail [raj]

But when **-il** is not final or does not follow a vowel, the [l] sound is indicated:

aile [ɛl]
péril [peril]

13.1 There are four exceptions (mentioned in Chapter I, Paragraph 2.4) in which **l** is simply a silent final consonant:

gentil	[ʒɑ̃ti]	sourcil	[sursi]
fusil	[fyzi]	outil	[uti]

REVIEW EXERCISES

The following exercises contain words spelled with **l** or **ll.** Distinguish carefully the pronunciation of **mille—ville—tranquille** and their derivatives from the vast majority of other similar spellings which have no [l] sound. A few words spelled with **l** or **ll** (see Paragraph 13) are introduced to offer practice in distinguishing them from the spellings representing the [j] sound.

A. Pronounce:

1. mille
2. la fille
3. la ville
4. il pille
   he pillages
5. tranquille
6. la famille
7. la cheville
   ankle
8. tranquillisant
9. jaillissant
   springing out
10. saillant
    projecting, salient
11. le village
12. le pillage
13. il mouille
    he moistens
14. mouillé
    moistened, wet
15. bouilli
    boiled
16. un million
17. le sillon
    furrow
18. le bouillon
19. un milliard
    billion
20. le vieillard
    old man

21. gaillard
 merry
22. vieille
23. l'ail
 garlic
24. l'aile
 wing
25. qu'il aille
 from aller
26. que tu ailles
 from aller
27. nous allions
28. le chandail
 sweater
29. meilleur
30. la paille
 straw
31. l'abeille
 bee
32. Marseille
33. l'œil
34. le fauteuil
 armchair
35. brouiller
 to jumble up
36. le brouillard
 fog
37. il brouille
38. il se débrouille
 he gets along
39. la grille
40. un millier
 about a thousand
41. la cédille
 cedilla
42. le réveil
 awakening
43. il réveille
 he awakens
44. la houille
 coal
45. veuillez
 please
46. il taille
 he carves
47. Chantilly
48. Neuilly
49. Auteuil
50. le seuil
 threshold
51. le maillot
 swimming trunks
52. la maille
 mesh
53. la ferraille
 scrap iron
54. la faillite
 bankruptcy
55. le carillon
56. la cuiller
 spoon (See Paragraph 2.1)
57. ailleurs
 elsewhere
58. d'ailleurs
 moreover
59. le bail
 lease
60. la vallée
 valley
61. qu'il vaille
 from valoir
62. l'aileron
 airplane flap
63. le vitrail
 stained glass window
64. le millionnaire
65. l'émail
 enamel
66. les coquilles
 shells

67. le millénaire
    millennium
68. la béquille
    crutch
69. l'artillerie
70. Guillaume
71. la Bastille
72. la bille
    billiard ball; marble
73. braille
    braille
74. Versailles
75. le cercueil
    coffin
76. le pilot
77. la guillotine
78. le bétail
    cattle
79. la quille
    keel
80. le billard
    billiards
81. sautiller
    to skip
82. s'agenouiller
    to kneel
83. les entrailles
    entrails, viscera
84. le corail
    coral
85. les semailles
    sowing
86. allié
    allied
87. l'orteil
    toe
88. ensoleillé
    sunny
89. bredouiller
    to stammer
90. le sérail
    harem

B. Pronounce:

1. une ville mouillée
2. des feuilles souillées
3. mille détails saillants
4. mille filles tranquilles
5. une bataille à Versailles
6. des milliers de treillis à Marseilles
7. une vieille abeille
8. un million de vieillards
9. un milliard de sillons
10. mille familles de chenilles tranquilles
11. Toutes les vieilles villes ont été pillées.
12. La grenouille se réveillait près des rails.
13. Elle était habillée de dentelles de Chantilly.
14. L'eau a failli bouillir.
15. Le vieillard était en deuil.
16. La volaille raille le petit oiseau parce que ses ailes sentent l'ail.

17. L'aile du vieil avion tombé a sillonné la surface tranquille de la terre.
18. Avez-vous vu la vieille vielle à Auteuil?
19. J'ai peur que cette aile ne lui aille pas bien.
20. Une chenille faisait tranquillement son chemin le long de la quille.
21. Il cueille des feuilles à Neuilly.
22. Il a raconté les détails saillants des représailles de Marseille et de Lille.
23. On veut que nous allions à Deauville avec Mireille et que lui y aille seul.
24. Dans la vallée, près du village, vivait tranquillement un vieil Allemand.
25. Les écailles d'émail scintillaient.

CHAPTER VI

THE NASAL VOWELS

14

The sounds of the French nasal vowels are usually not too difficult for American speakers of English to achieve. The problems are learning to associate French spellings with the proper nasals and learning where to avoid nasalization of a vowel standing next to an **m** or **n.**

The rule for nasalization can be reduced (with slight over-simplification) to this:

> A vowel is nasalized when it is followed by an **m** or an **n** in the same syllable. Exception: double **m** or double **n.**

This makes it necessary to know how to syllabicate. The rules are as follows:[1]

14.1 A single consonant between vowels goes with the vowel which follows it:

a-mi   di-gé-rer   ré-ci-té   ho-no-rons

The groups **ch, ph, th,** and **gn** represent single consonant sounds and always go with the vowel which follows:

sa-chons   sa-phir   ca-tho-de   sou-li-gner

14.2 Two consonants standing together are usually divided, one going with the preceding vowel, and one going with the following vowel:

ren-ver-sé   ar-tis-te   sen-ten-ce   ac-court

Doubled consonants are usually sounded as a single consonant and go with the syllable which follows:

accourt [a-kur]   année [a-ne]

If the second of two consonants is **l** or **r,** both consonants go with the vowel which follows:

é-clat   ac-ca-bler   é-cran   a-blu-tion

14.3 If three consonants occur together, the first goes with the preceding vowel and the others with the following vowel:

ab-ste-nir   mal-gré   dis-trait   rem-plir

EXERCISE

This exercise shows certain words divided into syllables. Pick out the syllables which would contain a nasal vowel, remembering that the vowel is nasal only when followed by **m** or **n** in the same syllable. Even then the vowel will not be nasalized if the **m** or **n** is doubled.

1. inanimé   i-na-ni-mé
2. onomatopée   o-no-ma-to-pé-e
3. honnête   hon-nê-te

[1] These are rules for the written language. Actual syllabication in speech is somewhat different, as observed by Professor Delattre in his book for l'École Française d'Été at Middlebury College. (Pierre Delattre, *Advanced Training in French Pronunciation* [Middlebury, Vermont: The College Store, 1949].)

4. innombrable	in-nom-bra-ble
5. ample	am-ple
6. unanime	u-na-ni-me
7. transir	tran-sir
8. nommer	nom-mer
9. nommons	nom-mons
10. enchantant	en-chan-tant
11. intimidation	in-ti-mi-da-tion
12. malin	ma-lin
13. intitulons	in-ti-tu-lons
14. maintenant	main-te-nant
15. inquiéter	in-quié-ter
16. constitution	con-sti-tu-tion
17. ronflons	ron-flons
18. enseignant	en-sei-gnant
19. ménager	mé-na-ger
20. ramoner	ra-mo-ner
21. tunnel	tun-nel
22. computation	com-pu-ta-tion
23. dynamique	dy-na-mi-que
24. penchant	pen-chant
25. involontaire	in-vo-lon-tai-re
26. magnanime	ma-gna-ni-me
27. intime	in-ti-me
28. synonyme	sy-no-ny-me
29. fine	fi-ne
30. une	u-ne

Note: In the last five examples above, the **mute e** at the end of a word counts as a pronounced vowel in syllabication. It is fully pronounced in singing if the next word begins with a consonant. In a similar position in verse it is counted as a syllable, although not clearly pronounced as in song. The **mute e** is also still sounded in some regional dialects. It formed a fully pronounced syllable during the centuries when habits of nasalization were being formed in the French language, and though not sounded now in standard spoken French, it still cancels the nasalizing effect of the preceding **m** or **n**.

15

There are four nasal vowels in standard French: [ɑ̃], [ɛ̃], [ɔ̃], [œ̃].

16

Spellings of the sound [ɑ̃]: The sound [ɑ̃] is represented by the four spellings **am, an, em, en.**

Examples:				
	champ	[ʃɑ̃]	temps	[tɑ̃]
	rampe	[rɑ̃p]	remplacer	[rɑ̃plase]
	tant	[tɑ̃]	tend	[tɑ̃]
	chanter	[ʃɑ̃te]	tente	[tɑ̃t]

EXERCISES

A. Pronounce the words in the following list. All of them contain one or more examples of [ɑ̃].

1. Adam
2. le champ
3. le camp
4. camper
5. tant
6. le chant
7. la chance
8. la plante
9. tremper
10. il trempe
11. remplir
12. sembler
13. cent
14. suspensif
15. gentil
16. la dentelle
17. ensemble
18. le chambranle
19. le tyran
20. le membre
21. ample
22. le sang
23. le pamphlet
24. penser
25. revendiquer
26. la quantité
27. tendre
28. le champagne
29. le semblant
30. la tempête

B. This exercise also illustrates words with the spellings **am, an, em, en,** but not all of them represent nasal vowels. Nasalize the vowel only when the **m** or **n** following it is in the same syllable and undoubled.

1. le champ
2. le camp
3. le hameçon
4. camper
5. le pamphlet
6. l'amateur
7. le pamplemousse
8. la lampe
9. laminer

10. dynamique
11. la famille
12. magnanime
13. le boulanger
14. il anime
15. tant
16. la tanne
17. la tanière
18. le chantier
19. Chanel
20. le franc
21. le flanc
22. le ban
23. bannir
24. banal
25. planter
26. planer
27. s'évanouir
28. l'évangile
29. l'âne
30. rembourser
31. premier
32. la température
33. sembler
34. semer
35. remuer
36. rembarquer
37. sentir
38. senestre
39. représentatif
40. il sent
41. la chenille
42. revendu
43. revenu
44. il ment
45. la menace
46. tendre
47. tenir
48. prendre
49. il prenne
50. le membre
51. la membrane
52. le chambranle
53. l'amande
54. le damier
55. la grammaire
56. l'épigramme
57. le sang
58. sanitaire
59. le segment
60. ramener

17 EXCEPTION

There is one exception to the rule that doubled **m** or **n** cancels the nasalization. Pronounce the following words as indicated by the phonetic symbols:

emmener	[ɑ̃mne]	ennuyer	[ɑ̃nɥije]
emmêler	[ɑ̃mɛle]	ennoblir	[ɑ̃nɔblir]

These words begin with a nasal vowel even though there is a double **m** or **n** in the spelling. The reason is that when **emm-** or **enn-** comes first in the word, it usually represents:

en + mener = emmener
en + mêler = emmêler
en + noble + ir = ennoblir

Ennuyer has a more complicated history, but receives the same treatment as the other words beginning **enn-**. There is one common word, however, which does not belong to this group:

ennemi [ɛnmi] *enemy*

17.1 Words like the following also have a nasal vowel in the first syllable:

enarbrer	[ɑ̃narbre]
enivrer	[ɑ̃nivre]
enorgueillir	[ɑ̃nɔrgœjir]

Here again **en-** figures as a prefix and retains its nasal vowel, contrary to the rules of nasalization formulated above. Notice that the **n** does double duty in that it indicates nasalization of the preceding vowel, but is also pronounced as a consonant.

18

In verb endings, make a careful distinction between the silent **-ent** of the third person plural and the participial ending **-ant** pronounced [ɑ̃].

Examples:	ils courent	[ilkur]
	en courant	[ɑ̃kurɑ̃]
	ils entrent	[ilzɑ̃tr]
	en entrant	[ɑ̃nɑ̃trɑ̃]
	ils en portent	[ilzɑ̃pɔrt]
	en portant	[ɑ̃pɔrtɑ̃]

EXERCISE

Pronounce the following phrases.

1. ils traduisent
   en traduisant
2. ils facilitent
   en facilitant
3. ils vendent
   en vendant
4. ils gesticulent
   en gesticulant
5. ils subissent
   en subissant
6. ils appellent
   en appelant [ɑ̃naplɑ̃]
7. elles souffrent
   en souffrant
8. elles arrangent
   en arrangeant
9. ils en ouvrent
   en ouvrant
10. ils en offrent
    en offrant

11. elles en comprennent
    en comprenant
12. ils s'en mêlent
    en s'en mêlant
13. ils s'aiment
    en s'aimant
14. ils certifient
    en certifiant
15. elles modifient
    en modifiant
16. ils se réconcilient
    en se réconciliant
17. ils se penchent
    en se penchant
18. elles chantent
    en chantant
19. ils gouvernent
    en gouvernant
20. ils y tiennent
    en y tenant

21. ils pendent — *they hang, are hanging*
    en pendant — *hanging*
    le pendant — *the pendant*
22. ils président — *they preside*
    en présidant — *while presiding*
    le président* — *the president*
23. ils précèdent — *they precede*
    en précédant — *preceding*
    le précédent* — *the precedent*

24. Les deux témoignages coïncident.
    The two bits of evidence coincide.

    un témoignage coïncident* avec l'autre
    one piece of evidence coinciding with the other

    deux figures coïncidentes
    two coinciding figures
25. un juriste éminent*

*The ending **-ent** is pronounced [ã] when it occurs in a noun or an adjective.

19

Spellings of the sound [ɔ̃]: The sound [ɔ̃] is represented by the spellings **om** or **on.**

EXERCISES

A. Pronounce the following words, each of which contains one or more nasal **o**'s.

1. le nom
2. les noms
3. le don
4. les dons
5. ils sont
6. il tombe
7. elle compte
8. qu'il rompe
9. nous fondons
10. le pompon
11. nous combinons
12. foncé
13. ils longent
14. le nonce
15. sombre
16. les combres
17. ils répondent
18. gonflé
19. le pilon
20. le ponton
21. les gonds
22. les joncs
23. nous montons
24. ils ronflent
25. nous comptons
26. j'annonce
27. le monde
28. nous longeons
29. vrombir
30. la fonte

B. This exercise also illustrates words with the spellings **-om-, -on-,** but they do not always indicate a nasal vowel.

1. le comble
2. compter
3. rompre
4. le nombre
5. fomenter
6. domestique
7. dominer
8. l'homme
9. l'hommage
10. le dommage
11. le plomb
12. le fond
13. la honte
14. long
15. son
16. honnête
17. l'honneur
18. nous ronflons
19. ramoner
20. l'onomatopée
21. le dom
22. nommer
23. le ronron
24. ronronner
25. il ronronne
26. la bombe
27. joncher
28. la monnaie
29. la sommation
30. nous tombons
31. le baron
32. la baronne
33. le polisson
34. la polissonne
35. Simon
36. Simone
37. le mouton
38. Domrémy
39. il connaît
40. la bonté

20

Spellings of the sound [œ̃]: The sound [œ̃] is represented by the spellings **um** and **un** (and in one case by **eun**).

EXERCISE

Pronounce the following words, distinguishing carefully between the nasalized **u** and the unnasalized **u.**

1. un [œ̃]
   une [yn]
2. lundi[2]
   la lune
3. aucun
   aucune
4. humble [œ̃bl]
   l'humilité
5. quelqu'un
   quelqu'une
6. le parfum
   il parfume
7. chacun
   chacune
8. commun
   commune
9. opportun
   opportune
10. importun
    importune
11. défunt
    le funiculaire
12. l'alun
    aluner
13. la rumeur
14. l'unité
15. le tunnel
16. fumer
17. puni
18. jeun [ʒœ̃]
19. Autun
20. Verdun

20.1 Borrowed words with the spelling **um** or **un** are usually not treated in the same way as native French words. Observe the pronunciation of the following borrowings from Latin.

album [albɔm]
maximum [maksimɔm]
minimum [minimɔm]

[2] Most Parisians, and many other French people, substitute [ɛ̃] for [œ̃]; *lundi* then sounds like *lindi*. This is still not uniform, uncontested usage, but students can expect to hear it often.

REVIEW EXERCISE

This exercise is a review of the three nasal sounds presented thus far, with additional practice in discriminating nasal from non-nasal vowels. There are many vowels in the following list of words which are not nasalized, though followed by an **m** or an **n.**

1. rencontrer
2. il rencontre
3. nommer
4. il nomme
5. la nomenclature
6. l'ensemble
7. le sentiment
8. sentimental
9. lombard
10. dominer
11. nous dominons
12. fomenter
13. nous fomentâmes
14. fumant
15. un parfum
16. un pompon
17. la pomme
18. la gomme
19. le gond
20. l'hexagone
21. l'ennemi
22. ennuyer
23. j'ennuie
24. emménager
25. j'emménage
26. la lune
27. lundi
28. ruminant
29. le son
30. il sonne
31. le ton
32. il tonne
33. le vent
34. il vend
35. qu'il vende
36. la vente
37. la viande
38. il se vante
39. bon
40. bonne
41. Bône
42. il comprend
43. qu'il comprenne
44. nous comprenons
45. vous comprenez
46. le chignon
47. il commande
48. le compliment
49. le compromis
50. monotone

21

Spellings of the sound [ɛ̃]: The nasal vowel [ɛ̃] is spelled **aim, ain, eim, ein, im, in, ym, yn**; it is also spelled **en** in the endings **-ien, -yen, -éen** (**ien** may appear in certain verb forms: *v**ien**drai*). It is also the vowel sound in **oin,** pronounced [wɛ̃].

EXERCISES

A. The following list consists of words containing the nasal vowel [ɛ̃] in one or more syllables.

1. la faim
2. Paimpol
3. le daim
4. la main
5. le nain
6. sain

7. craint
8. la crainte
9. mainte
10. saint
11. sainte
12. le pain
13. le refrain
14. certain
15. il plaint
16. napolitain
17. le grain
18. la plainte
19. tu crains
20. Reims [rɛ̃s]
21. le sein
22. serein
23. j'éteins
24. tu éteins
25. il éteint
26. il teint
27. il peint
28. tu peins
29. je feins
30. il feint
31. ceint
32. éreinté
33. je feindrai
34. tu éteindras
35. il peindra
36. vous teindrez
37. simple
38. le timbre
39. la timbale
40. limpide
41. implorer
42. impossible
43. le pin
44. le lin
45. le linge
46. la meringue [mərɛ̃g]
47. la seringue
48. le serin
49. il pince
50. rincer
51. le matin
52. divin
53. libertin
54. Chopin
55. Martin
56. marin
57. il vint
58. je tins
59. tu tins
60. il tint
61. nous vînmes [vɛ̃m]
62. nous tînmes [tɛ̃m]
63. juin
64. l'injustice
65. indigne
66. installer
67. l'insecte
68. intangible
69. inventer
70. j'invente
71. nous inventons
72. le symbole
73. la symphonie
74. la sympathie
75. la lymphe
76. la syntaxe
77. la synthèse
78. le lynx [lɛ̃ks]
79. le labyrinthe
80. bien
81. rien
82. je viens
83. il vient
84. il tient
85. le tien
86. le mien
87. le sien
88. les tiens
89. les siens
90. les miens
91. chrétien
92. parisien
93. italien
94. moyen
95. le doyen
96. méditerranéen
97. européen
98. le coin
99. loin
100. l'examen [ɛgzamɛ̃]*

*There are a few words borrowed from Latin in which the spelling **en** is pronounced [ɛ̃]. *Examen* is the most common one.

B. This exercise is intended to give you practice in making the instantaneous adjustment to the non-nasal vowel in the final syllable when you see the **mute e** added to the **n.**

Nasal Vowels · 21

1. marin [marɛ̃]
   marine [marin]
2. libertin [libɛrtɛ̃]
   libertine [libɛrtin]
3. le cousin [kuzɛ̃]
   la cousine [kuzin]
4. fin
   fine
5. bovin
   bovine
6. Martin
   Martine
7. clandestin
   clandestine
8. Paulin
   Pauline
9. divin
   divine
10. limousin
    limousine
11. Chopin
    la chopine
12. le pin
    il opine
13. mesquin
    mesquine
14. l'assassin
    il assassine
15. le coquin
    la coquine
16. le jardin
    il jardine
17. le magasin
    le magazine
18. l'orphelin
    l'orpheline
19. le baragouin
    il baragouine
20. sain [sɛ̃]
    saine [sɛn]
21. la main [mɛ̃]
    le Maine [mɛn]
22. le train
    il traîne
23. le grain
    la graine
24. plain
    plaine
    qu'il plaigne [plɛɲ]
25. américain
    américaine
26. mexicain
    mexicaine
27. serein
    sereine
28. plein
    pleine
29. le sein
    la Seine
30. le mien [mjɛ̃]
    la mienne [mjɛn]
31. le tien [tjɛ̃]
    la tienne [tjɛn]
32. le sien
    la sienne
33. chrétien
    chrétienne
34. parisien
    parisienne
35. européen
    européenne
36. méditerranéen
    méditerranéenne
37. moins [mwɛ̃]
    le moine [mwan]
38. le soin
    il soigne [swaɲ]
39. il joint
    qu'il joigne
40. le foin
    Antoine

21.1 Like other final consonants, a final **n** is silent although its presence indicates the nasalization of the preceding vowel. Like other final consonants, it is to be pronounced whenever a **mute e** is added at the end of the word.

21.2 The **im-** or **in-** in the initial position needs some special attention. The prefix indicates the nasal vowel only when followed by a consonant:

in-strument [ɛ̃strymɑ̃] in-time [ɛ̃tim]

Obeying the usual rule about doubling of the consonant, the prefix is not nasal in words beginning with **imm-** or **inn-**:

im-mense [imɑ̃s] in-nocence [inɔsɑ̃s]

The initial syllable is not nasal when a vowel follows the **m** or **n**:

i-miter [imite] i-nachevé [inaʃve]

EXERCISE

Divide each of the following words into syllables, and pronounce, giving special attention to the nasal or non-nasal quality of the first syllable.

1. instable
2. l'injure
3. l'insistence
4. l'inscription
5. importer
6. impressif
7. l'impôt
8. imprimer
9. infini
10. injecter
11. immédiat
12. immatériel
13. immobile
14. immodeste
15. immonde
16. innombrable
17. l'innovation
18. innocent
19. l'immensité
20. l'innocuité
21. l'image
22. imiter
23. j'imite
24. inacceptable
25. inachevé
26. l'inadvertance
27. inadmissible
28. l'inanité
29. inédit
30. inefficace
31. inégal
32. inexorable
33. inexplicable
34. l'inondation
35. inorganique
36. indécis
37. inutile
38. inhumain [inymɛ̃]
39. inimaginable
40. l'inimité
41. initial
42. instituer
43. l'instance
44. inhiber
45. insérer
46. j'injecte
47. il immole
48. l'instruction
49. inofficiel
50. l'instigation
51. impossible
52. immoral
53. l'impact
54. immaculé
55. imitative

56. à l'insu
57. inopportun
58. intrinsèque
59. inintelligible
60. ininterrompu
61. impeccable
62. une injure inacceptable
63. une inondation inouïe
64. les impôts inexorables
65. une innovation inefficace
66. l'inspiration immédiate
67. l'infinité immense
68. l'intensité inhérente
69. l'insistence ininterrompue
70. On insère un instrument inoxydable.

REVIEW EXERCISE

This is another exercise to give practice in pronouncing the final syllable correctly. It is similar to Exercise B under Paragraph 21, but uses all the nasal vowels. The order of the pairs is varied.

1. le nom
   il nomme
2. le dom
   le dôme
3. divin
   divine
4. malsain
   malsaine
5. commun
   commune
6. il parfume
   le parfum
7. le plan
   il plane
8. l'âne
   l'an
9. Simon
   Simone
10. le rein
    la reine
11. le gazon
    il gazonne
12. féminine
    féminin
13. aucun
    aucune
14. les tiennes
    les tiens
15. les Cubains
    les Cubaines
16. les Napolitaines
    les Napolitains
17. les Alpines
    les Alpins
18. les orphelins
    les orphelines
19. les baronnes
    les barons
20. les siens
    les siennes
21. le bassin
    la bassine
22. le domaine
    demain
23. les Méditerranéennes
    les Méditerranéens
24. dominicain
    dominicaine
25. le pan
    la panne
26. jeune
    à jeun
    le jeûne
27. le parrain
    la marraine
28. chacune
    chacun
29. le poison
    il empoisonne
30. brun
    brune
31. l'emprunt
    la prune
32. certaine
    certain
33. le mouton
    il moutonne
34. le soupçon
    soupçonneux
35. l'éperon
    il éperonne

CHAPTER VII

AI and AY

22

The **ai** (**aî**) in French stands for the closed sound [e] and the open sound [ɛ]. These are the same two sounds (approximately) that it represents in English—for example, in *maid* and *hair*. There is some variation among the French-speaking peoples of Europe with regard to the use of the closed or the open sound, but the simplest rule is to follow the practice of the majority of the French: Pronounce [e] in an open syllable, particularly at the end of a word; [ɛ] in a closed syllable.

Open syllables (those ending in a vowel sound)	*Closed syllables (those ending in a consonant sound)*
1. gai	1. la fraise
2. je sais[1]	2. laide
3. je ferai	3. j'aime
4. laid[1]	4. il aide
5. le palais[1]	5. la fournaise
6. je donnai	6. la laine
7. je donnerai	7. le maire
8. je donnerais[1]	8. raide
9. je paie[1]	9. vaine
10. il connaît[1]	10. faible

22.1 When the **ai** is at the end of the word, it must not be allowed to become the diphthong of similar English words. Pronounce the following pairs, making the clear distinction between the French vowel and the English diphthong.

[1] In words like these, most dictionaries and textbooks conservatively show an **open e,** but practically all Frenchmen pronounce instead a **closed e.** The same is true for words ending in **-et, -êt**: *complet, bouquet*. The **closed e** is adopted in this manual because it hardly seems useful to teach students rules of pronunciation which the French do not usually follow. The **closed e** in these cases is *la prononciation la plus naturelle des gens cultivés,* as noted by Professor Delattre in his work on French phonetics. (Pierre Delattre, *Principes de Phonétique Française* 2nd ed. [Middlebury, Vermont: Middlebury College École Française d'Été, 1961].)

French		*English*	
gai	[ge]	gay	[ge^i]
plaie	[ple]	play	[ple^i]
mai	[me]	may	[me^i]
sais	[se]	say	[se^i]
raie	[re]	ray	[re^i]

22.2 Sometimes the spelling **ay** is simply a varient of **ai**—for example in *Douay, Épernay, je paye* (*=je paie*). But when **ay** is followed by a pronounced vowel the sound indicated is [ɛj].

Examples:
1. ayant
2. nous essayons
3. vous essayez
4. balayer
5. je payai
6. les rayons

EXERCISE

Pronounce:

1. gai
2. le geai
3. mai
4. il plaît
5. je parlai
6. je jetai
7. je jetais
8. je jetterai
9. je jetterais
10. il ferait
11. j'ai
12. tu sais
13. mais
14. l'aile
15. française
16. le questionnaire
17. il paraissait
18. la falaise
19. il saisissait
20. anglaise
21. pair
22. clair
23. faire
24. qu'il taise
25. il essayait
26. il balayait
27. nous essayons
28. ils payaient
29. la raie
30. la plaie
31. il donnerait
32. il se tait
33. je connais
34. il reconnaît
35. Calais
36. payé
37. je serrais
38. la grammaire
39. épais
40. baisser

23

The rules and examples which follow specify instances in which **ai** and **ay** represent sounds other than the closed sound [e] and the open sound [ɛ] discussed in the preceding paragraphs.

23.1 **Ai** is pronounced [ə] in the following forms of the verb ***faire:***

Present Participle:	faisant [ə]	
1st Pers. Pl. Present:	nous faisons [ə]	
Imperfect Indicative:	je faisais [ə]	nous faisions [ə]
	tu faisais [ə]	vous faisiez [ə]
	il faisait [ə]	ils faisaient [ə]

This pronunciation of **ai** applies to all the corresponding forms of the compounds of ***faire:***

défaire	*to undo*	satisfaire	*to satisfy*
contrefaire	*to counterfeit*	*etc.*	

And also to all nouns and adjectives derived from the present participial form of ***faire:***

faisable	*feasible*	le faiseur	*maker, doer*
la malfaisance	*malfeasance*		

23.2 In the following few words the **ay** stands for [ei]:

Examples:	le pays	[pei]	*country*
	le paysage	[peizaʒ]	*countryside, landscape*
	le paysan	[peizɑ̃]	*peasant*
	l'abbaye	[abei]	*abbey*

23.3 Followed by **m** or **n** in the same syllable, the **ai** is nasalized. (See Paragraph 21.)

Examples:	la faim	la plainte
	sain	la main
	craint	

23.4 There are cases where the **a** and **i** fall into juxtaposition but obey other rules. When **ai** is followed by a final **l** or by **-ll-** in the middle of the word, the **i** is to be interpreted as going with the **l** to indicate the sound [j]. (See Chapter V.)

Examples:	le travail	qu'il aille
	le rail	Versailles
	le détail	

23.5 The diaeresis over the **i** indicates that it is to be separated from the **a,** each letter then maintaining its usual separate value. (See Paragraphs 45.1 and 45.2.)

Examples:	le maïs	[mais]
	naïf	[naif]
	naïve	[naiv]
	aïe	[ai]
	Thaïs	[tais]
	l'aïeul[2]	[ajœl]

REVIEW EXERCISE

All the pronunciations of **ai, ay** are illustrated in this exercise.

1. le quai
2. vrai
3. le rabais
4. je paye
5. saine
6. sain
7. l'abbaye
8. raide
9. le rail
10. il serait
11. le sérail
12. la paie
13. le pays
14. nous faisions
15. nous plaisions
16. la paillasse
17. le maïs
18. qu'ils aillent
19. la faïence
20. faiblir
21. infaillible
22. gai
23. gaillard
24. la gaine
25. égayer
26. ils faisaient
27. pair
28. le pain
29. le rayon
30. il paillait
31. le faisan *pheasant*
32. il payait
33. le paysage
34. en faisant
35. la braise
36. essayant
37. la faillite du paysan
38. un païen malfaisant
39. Elle l'essaierait gaîment.
40. Je sais les détails de l'affaire du maïs.

[2] This illustrates the principle that **i** or **y,** when followed by a vowel, represents the sound [j]. Confer Paragraph 22.2 above.

CHAPTER VIII

OPEN O AND CLOSED O

24

French has the **open o** [ɔ] and the **closed o** [o]. The **open o** is by far the more common sound, but the tendency of native English speakers learning French is to overwork the closed sound, especially in cognates. A practical way to approach the problem is to memorize the spellings that are pronounced [o], then give the sound [ɔ] to all other occurrences of **o.** The [ɔ] is approximately the vowel in the English *cloth, lost.*

EXERCISES

A. This exercise contains cognates, all of which have the **open o** in French. Be careful to avoid the **closed o** of the English equivalent, which is identical or similar in spelling.

1. la note
2. le vote
3. la romance
4. roquefort
5. la proportion
6. prolonger
7. provoquer
8. noble
9. il adore
10. le croquet
11. le crochet
12. la nomenclature
13. incohérent
14. baroque
15. le cobra
16. ovale
17. le motif
18. la locomotive
19. la rotation
20. la tomate
21. la topaze
22. d'abord
23. l'odeur
24. l'opinion
25. la phobie *phobia*
26. implorer
27. opaque
28. le mode
29. posséder
30. portugais

B. Continue with the following cognates. The English equivalents give a variety of treatments to the **o,** but you should pronounce it [ɔ] in all these French words.

1. exotique	8. l'honneur	15. politique
2. scolaire	9. dominer	16. le pilote
3. la monnaie	10. la force	17. l'objet
4. le bonnet	11. l'estomac	18. obtenir
5. il pardonne	12. le docteur	19. octobre
6. officiel	13. le sport	20. modeste
7. la période	14. le soldat	

25

The **closed o** is the sound used:

(a) When it is the final sound in the word;
(b) For **ô;**
(c) When spelled **o + s + vowel;**
(d) **O + tion;**
(e) For **au** and **eau.**

(a) Final sound:	*(b) O circumflex:*	*(c) O + S + Vowel:*
1. Hugo	1. tôt	1. poser
2. le mécano	2. l'hôte	2. la pose
3. clos	3. l'hôtel	3. la prose
4. le dos	4. le côté	4. la dose
5. les os	5. le dôme	5. le gosier
6. les mots	6. rôti	6. la rose
7. le fagot	7. le nôtre	7. rosée
8. les flots	8. Bône	8. il expose
9. le maillot	9. la tôle	9. l'exposition
10. le sirop	10. la clôture	10. la chose

(d) O + -tion:	*(e) Spelled au:*	*Spelled eau:*
1. la lotion	1. le taux	1. beau
2. la motion	2. chauve	2. la beauté
3. la notion	3. mauve	3. l'eau
4. la potion	4. il faut	4. la peau
5. la dévotion	5. la pause	5. le plateau
6. l'émotion	6. la fraude	6. le trousseau
7. la commotion	7. l'échafaud	7. Deauville
8. commotionner	8. causer	8. le chapiteau
9. émotionnable	9. la paume	9. les châteaux
10. la locomotion	10. égaux	10. le manteau

25.1 Note exceptions to (e) above: **Au + r** is given the **open o** sound as illustrated in the following examples.

1. j'aurai [ɔre]
   tu auras [ɔra]
   etc.
2. je saurai [sɔre]
   tu sauras [sɔra]
   etc.
3. le laurier [lɔrje]

Another miscellaneous exception is the proper noun *Paul* [pɔl].

25.2 Words spelled **o + ss** have sometimes [o], sometimes [ɔ], and do not conform to any pattern. For example:

1. la fosse [fos]
2. grosse [gros]
   masc. gros [gro]
3. le dossier [dosje]

1. brosser [brɔse]
2. la bosse [bɔs]
3. le gosse [gɔs]

25.3 Certain other spellings yield sometimes [o], sometimes [ɔ]—for example **-om-, -on-**. Moreover, the choice of vowel for certain words varies with individual French speakers. This discussion aims to give the main outlines of usage and to emphasize that the open sound is the more frequent one.

26

Although more specifically a phonetic problem, it should be pointed out that neither the [o] nor the [ɔ] is exactly like its English counterpart; particularly in the case of the closed sound, the diphthongizing [oᵘ] of English should be avoided.

EXERCISES

A. In each of the following pairs of words of similar spelling, only one of the words contains the [o].

1. le pilot
   le pilote
2. la cote
   la côte
3. notre
   nôtre

4. la poste
   la pose
5. le dos
   la dot
6. crotté
   le côté
7. vôtre
   votre
8. le picot
   le picotage
9. la rose
   le rostre
10. le môme
    la momie
11. le pot
    le potage
12. la botte
    le jabot
13. le chômage
    le chocolat
14. total
    tantôt
15. la paume
    la pomme
16. le gosier
    le gosse
17. la fosse
    la brosse
18. jaune
    le pigeonnier
19. l'argot
    argoter
20. la taupe
    nous saurons

B. Each of the following words contains both sounds of **o.**

1. le domino
2. les propos
3. le folio
4. le coquelicot
5. le taureau
6. le rocambeau
7. le tonneau
8. totaux
9. le vol-au-vent
10. Trocadéro

C. The list below contains a random mixture of words containing **open** and **closed o**'s.

1. austère
2. la paupière
3. l'aurore
4. sauf
5. l'apôtre
6. économe
7. le coffre
8. l'opéra
9. le bloc
10. le col
11. le roc
12. l'escroc (*final consonant silent*)
13. le bol
14. le globe
15. sobre
16. l'étoffe
17. l'ode
18. l'époque
19. drôle
20. le fantôme
21. le Rhône
22. l'Écosse
23. arroser
24. l'abricot
25. inodore
26. sonore
27. coloniser
28. l'ilôt
29. le polygone
30. polyglotte
31. le restaurant
32. la parole
33. les moineaux
34. le coq d'or
35. le gros lot

CHAPTER IX

GN

27

The **gn** in French stands for a sound approximately like the **ny** in the English *canyon*. As produced in French, this sound is a single consonant represented by the symbol [ɲ].

EXERCISE

Pronounce the following words, all of which contain the consonant combination **gn.**

1. la ligne
2. le signe
3. ignorer
4. j'ignore
5. gagner
6. il gagne
7. magnifique
8. l'agneau
9. Agnès (*final consonant pronounced*)
10. ils se résignent
11. mignon
12. signaler
13. le champignon
14. qu'il plaigne
15. elle feignait
16. poignant
17. elles peignent
18. dédaigner
19. il joignait
20. l'ignominie
21. ignoble
22. clignoter
23. le témoignage
24. il rogne
25. le chignon
26. la poignée
27. l'indignation
28. indigne
29. magnanime
30. le renseignement
31. magnétique
32. la vignette
33. la vigne
34. la bagnole
35. imprégné

CHAPTER X

QU

28

Qu = [k] in most French words. This pronunciation is even rather common in English in the host of words borrowed from French: *oblique, unique, antique, burlesque, grotesque, croquette, liqueur, queue,* etc.

EXERCISE

Pronounce the following list of words which all exhibit the sound [k] spelled **qu.**

1. qui
2. que
3. le quai
4. le croquet
5. la croquette
6. grotesque
7. oblique
8. la claque
9. piquant
10. le banquet
11. qualifier
12. la quenille
13. la séquence
14. le sequin
15. coquet
16. coquette
17. équivalent
18. la liqueur
19. inquiet
20. burlesque
21. obséquieux
22. le tourniquet
23. cynique
24. Québec
25. la queue
26. quotidien
27. Quentin
28. critique
29. unique
30. antique
31. la quincaillerie
32. inique
33. l'iniquité
34. la bique
35. moqueuse
36. la torque
37. la fréquence
38. intrinsèque
39. l'aqueduc
40. le reliquaire

Note: Although some French words show **qu** having its English (and Latin and Italian) value of [kw], they are mostly learned or less common words not needed in a beginner's vocabulary, and they can be acquired later. The main problem at first is to cease attributing the English value of this combination to its appearance in French words.

CHAPTER XI

G and GU

29

G is hard before **a, o,** and **u** in French; soft before **e, i,** and **y.** A moment's reflection will show that the same rule operates in English—for example: (hard) *game, dragon, gull, pagan;* (soft) *gem, regent, sage, register, gin, gymnasium.* (English has a few exceptions: *begin, get,* etc.; French has no exceptions.) In both languages **g** is hard before a consonant.

EXERCISE

Pronounce:

1. les bagages
2. le magasin
3. gaulois
4. le gaz
5. le ragout
6. le bigot
7. égayer
8. guttural
9. grand
10. global
11. figé
12. l'âge
13. le régent
14. l'apogée
15. geler
16. étrange
17. le régiment
18. la gynécologie
19. fugitif
20. le régime

30

The soft sound of **g** [ʒ], can be indicated even before **a, o,** and **u** by the spelling **ge.** The **e** is just a spelling device and has no pronunciation.[1]

[1] The **soft g** in English is not the same as the **soft g** in French. The **g** in English *gymnasium* is phonetically [dʒ], whereas the **g** of **gymnase** is [ʒ]. But the French soft sound for the **g** is also well represented in English in a number of borrowings from the French. Examples: *beige, corsage, cortege, espionage, garage, sabotage.*

EXERCISE
Pronounce:

1. nous mangeons
2. nous mangeâmes
3. vous mangeâtes
4. Georges
5. je songeais
6. je mangeai
7. j'engageai
8. nous engageons
9. songeant
10. engageant
11. nous bougeons
12. bougeant
13. vous bougeâtes
14. le geai
15. le cageot
16. nous figeons
17. ils figeaient
18. nous interrogeons
19. ils interrogeaient
20. nous interrogeâmes

Note: This spelling occurs most often in the forms of verbs such as ***manger, songer, bouger.*** The **soft g** of the infinitive stem is retained throughout all forms of the verb. This is indicated by the spelling **ge** whenever the ending begins with an **a** or an **o.** Notice that English uses the same device in *mana**ge**able*, ***George***, *ser**ge**ant*, *sur**ge**on*, etc.

31

The use of **gu** before an **e** or **i** in French indicates retention of the hard sound.

EXERCISE
Pronounce:

1. la guêpe
2. le guichet
3. le guide
4. guetter
5. aux aguets
6. la digue
7. le dogue
8. la ligue
9. le monologue
10. la vogue

Note: Though English is less consistent, it has many examples of the same spelling device: *guess, guide, league, monologue, morgue,* etc.

32

There are a few French words spelled with a **gu** in which the **u** represents a separate sound. The commonest three are probably the following:

aigu, aiguë	[egy]	*sharp, pointed, acute*
l'aiguille	[egɥij]	*needle; hand (of a clock)*
linguistique	[lɛ̃gɥistik]	*linguistic*

The diaeresis on the feminine form ***aiguë*** is to indicate that the **u** is fully pronounced, as in the masculine, and that the **gue** is not to be pronounced as in *bague, vogue,* etc. (See Paragraph 45.3.)

Most of the words derived from ***aigu, aiguille,*** have a pronounced **u.** Study the list in the dictionary.

REVIEW EXERCISE

The list of words below illustrates the pronunciations of **g** and **gu** discussed in this chapter.

1. le linge
   la lingue
2. il longe
   longue
3. lige
   la ligue
4. la langue
   le lange
5. la vigueur
   la vigile
6. longer
   la longueur
7. ingurgiter
   ingérer
   inguérissable
8. le gilet
   le guillemet
9. Gide
   le guide
10. le dogue
    le doge
11. le virage
    la virago
12. rogue
    Roger
13. rougir
    rougeâtre
    la rougeole
    rougeaud
14. la fougasse
    la fougeraie
15. la fougue
    la fougère
16. mugir
    le muguet
17. la guenille
    le genêt
18. la guenon
    nous gênons
19. légal
    légitime
20. le ragoût
    rageur
    rager
    raguer
21. la gerbe
    la guerre

22. indigo
    indigène
    indigéré
    indigne
23. léger
    léguer
24. la loge
    le monologue
25. courageux
    la baguette
26. le collège
    le collègue
27. alléger
    alléguer
28. Georges
    la gorge
29. gai
    le geai
30. l'orge
    l'orgue
31. Guillaume
    fragile
32. Peugeot
    gothique
33. le fourgon
    le bourgeon
34. le golfe
    le geôlier
35. une aiguille
36. un accent aigu
37. une douleur aiguë
38. le Tage
39. la toge
40. dégingandé

CHAPTER XII

TH

33

The **th** in French always represents simply the sound (t). It must never be given the English sound.

EXERCISE

Pronounce the following words:

1. le thème
2. la thèse
3. la thérapie
4. thérapeutique
5. thermal
6. la théorie
7. le thé
8. la théologie
9. le théoricien
10. la théosophie
11. le thon
12. le mythe
13. le labyrinthe
14. bath [bat]
15. l'esthète
16. esthétique
17. Pathé
18. la pathologie
19. le pathologiste
20. catholique
21. l'éther [etɛr]

22. éthique
23. ethnique
24. l'Éthiopie
25. la cathédrale
26. Athènes [atɛn]
27. les Athéniens
28. l'arithmétique
29. enthousiaste
30. l'hypothèse
31. le stéthoscope
32. le théâtre
33. pathétique
34. la synthèse
35. le rythme
36. rythmique
37. l'athée
38. la parenthèse
39. Château-Thierry
40. Mithridate
41. l'athlète
42. la sympathie
43. Macbeth
44. Élizabeth
45. Ruth
46. l'apathie
47. le zénith
48. l'épithète
49. l'orthographe
50. l'orthodontiste

Note: The **th** is silent in ***l'asthme*** and ***l'isthme,*** as in English *asthma* and *isthmus.*

CHAPTER XIII

T=S

34

The **t** of the spelling **ti** or **tie** may sound as [s] or [t]. It indicates [s] in the words whose English cognate has [ʃ] or [s]. It indicates [t] where there is a [t] in the English equivalent.

Examples:	*French*		*English*
	nation	[nɑsjɔ̃]	nation
	mention	[mɑ̃sjɔ̃]	mention
	partial	[parsjal]	partial
	initié	[inisje]	initiated *or* initiate (*adj.*)
	diplomatie	[diplomasi]	diplomacy
But:	pitié	[pitje]	pity
	modestie	[mɔdɛsti]	modesty

EXERCISE

Pronounce:

1. mention	26. action
2. prévention	27. imitation
3. attrition	28. partie
4. notion	29. tradition
5. potion	30. différentier
6. friction	31. substantiel
7. fiction	32. spatial
8. organisation	33. distinction
9. exagération	34. initial
10. fermentation	35. facétieux *facetious*
11. essentiel	36. garantie *guarantee*
12. section	37. inertie *inertia*
13. déclaration	38. prophétie *prophecy*
14. injection	39. initié
15. partial	40. initiation
16. nation	41. vénitien
17. insatiable	42. description
18. pitié	43. sortie
19. aristocratie	44. amitié *amity, friendship*
20. aviation	45. autocratie
21. discrétion	46. théocratie
22. coalition	47. suprématie *supremacy*
23. démocratie	48. intention
24. modestie	49. dérivation
25. diplomatie	50. pénitentiaire

35

The sound [sj] in French requires particular attention because the English speaker has the habit of blending these sounds into [ʃ]. For example, *nation* is pronounced "*nashun*", *partial* is pronounced "*parshal*", etc. This happens even in adjoining words in English: *this year* is often pronounced "*thishear*". This tendency must be avoided in French, and the [sj] in words like *conversa**tion**, pas**sion**, le **sien*** must be kept very clear and unambiguous. Practice contrasting the two sounds in the following columns:

[sj]	[ʃ]
nous cassions	nous cachons
conversation	sachions
partial	par châles
le sien	le chien

CHAPTER XIV

B=P

36

B is pronounced [p] when it occurs before **s** or **t** as illustrated in the following exercise.

EXERCISE

Pronounce:

1. l'observation
2. l'observatoire
3. observer
4. j'observe
5. nous observons
6. obscurcir
7. l'obscurcissement
8. obséder
9. l'obsession
10. obscure
11. obtempérer
12. l'obstruction
13. obtus
14. obscène
15. obstétrique
16. obtenir
17. j'obtiens
18. il obtient
19. obstiner
20. ils s'obstinent
21. substantier
22. la substance
23. l'obstacle
24. abstrait
25. abstenir
26. on abstient
27. absurde
28. la substitution
29. l'absence
30. absolu

CHAPTER XV

CH

37

The more common pronunciation of **ch** in French is [ʃ], which is the sound given to **sh** in English. The French sound for **ch,** however, is well known in English because of the many borrowings from French. For example, pronounce the following as English words: *chef*, *Chevrolet*, *chauffeur*, *echelon*, *brochure*, *chaperon*, *moustache*, *touché*, *chic*, *ricochet.*

EXERCISE

Pronounce the following French words.

1. l'archevêque
2. l'architecte
3. l'architecture
4. les archives
5. achever
6. le bachelier
7. le bachot
8. la brochure
9. le charme
10. le chef
11. cacher
12. le crochet
13. le chaperon
14. chauffer
15. le chauffeur
16. la douche
17. l'échelon
18. fâché
19. la fiche
20. la moustache
21. la niche
22. ricocher
23. sécher
24. toucher
25. la ruche
26. Vichy
27. Rochefort
28. acharné
29. achever
30. mâchonner

38

Many words of Greek origin give the sound [k] to the **ch.** The following list illustrates such words. Notice that the words listed below all have an English cognate which gives the same sound to the **ch.**

1. l'archéologie
2. l'archéologue
3. l'archaïsme
4. le chaos [kao]
5. le chœur *chorus, choir*
6. chrétien
7. l'orchestre
8. l'écho
9. la psychanalyse [psikanaliz]
10. le psychiâtre [psikiɑtr]

One guide to determining which occurrences of **ch** are pronounced [k] is this: If the English cognate uses the sound [k], do the same in French, with the exception of the following common words (and their derivatives), in which French has softened the **ch** to a [ʃ]:

Achille [aʃil]
l'architecte
le catéchisme
la hiérarchie
la monarchie
le patriarche

CHAPTER XVI

39

The **h** appears in several digraphs such as **ch** and **th,** which have already been discussed. Here we are studying the **h** alone, which appears in many words and is always silent. Ignore it in pronunciation and treat the surrounding letters as if the **h** were not there.

EXERCISE

Pronounce the following words:

1. l'hôtel
2. la silhouette
3. déshonorer
4. déshabiller
5. habiller
6. habiter
7. Anouilh
8. il hait
9. l'honneur
10. l'humeur
11. Mulhouse
12. inhérent
13. inhabile
14. le souhait
15. inhumain
16. incompréhensible
17. le véhicule
18. adhérent
19. l'adhésion
20. prohiber
21. le bonhomme
22. dehors
23. exhalé
24. le bonheur
25. le malheur
26. le brouhaha
27. la cohorte
28. le cahier
29. trahir
30. la cohésion
31. exhaustif
32. envahir
33. l'envahisseur
34. abhorrer
35. la véhémence

40

Although the **h** is always silent, some words begin with the so-called **aspirate h** which has the effect of preventing linking and elision. Like the **mute h,** the **aspirate h** is silent, although it was still being sounded in the centuries when habits of linking and elision were being formed. It is usually indicated in the dictionary by an apostrophe or an asterisk. Some of the commonest words which display an **aspirate h** are the following: *huit, héros, hors-d'œuvre, haut, honte, haïr, hasard, hall.*

EXERCISE

Pronounce the following words and phrases, each of which contains an **aspirate h.**

1. le huit mars
2. les huit hommes
3. en haut
4. les terres hautes
5. je le hais
6. je les hais
7. elle la hait
8. elle les hait
9. le héros
10. les héros
11. la honte
12. les hontes
13. le hasard
14. les hasards
15. le hall
16. les halls
17. le Hollandais
18. les Hollandais
19. le Hongrois
20. les Hongrois

CHAPTER XVII

OU

41

The **ou** and **oû** represent the sound [u] in French. It indicates this sound even in a number of English words such as *you, group,* or such borrowings from French as *routine, troupe.* But in French it must not be allowed to become a different sound when followed by **r,** as happens in English. For example, the vowel of ***tourner*** must not be influenced by English *turn,* or ***touriste*** by *tourist.*

EXERCISE

Pronounce:

1. le coup
2. court
3. le courant
4. il pousse
5. pour
6. goûter
7. le gourmet
8. mourir
9. la moue
10. bourrer
11. il bourre
12. bouder
13. toucher
14. tourner
15. il touche
16. il tourne
17. le coucou
18. couvert
19. la loupe
20. lourd

42

The **ou** followed by a pronounced vowel becomes the semi-consonant [w], as exemplified in the following exercise.

EXERCISE

Pronounce:

1. oui
2. ouest
3. l'ouate
4. jouer
5. nous jouons
6. doué
7. inouï
8. la silhouette
9. la douane
10. boueux
11. la louange
12. le souhait

REVIEW EXERCISE

Pronounce the following words and phrases which illustrate the two pronunciations of **ou.**

1. il a tourné
2. il a joué
3. nous nouons
4. vous nouez
5. vous nourrissez
6. il est pourri
7. le poulet
8. le courage
9. c'est bourré
10. le gourmet
11. le gourmand
12. la tournée
13. la toupée
14. la gouache
15. gouailler
16. pouilleux [pujø]
17. pouah!
18. le touage
19. ils courent
20. le bourreau
21. fourrer
22. la joue
23. le jour
24. s'agenouiller
25. Oui, il pousse vers l'ouest.

CHAPTER XVIII

SILENT LETTERS OTHER THAN IN FINAL POSITION

43

There are a few silent letters other than in final position. The **p** is silent in the families of words derived from ***baptiser, compter, dompter, exempter, sculpter, prompt.*** The **m** is silent in ***automne,*** in ***damner*** and its derivatives (but not in other occurrences of **mn:** *indemniser, amnistie, hymne,* etc.) Further individual cases of silent letters occur in the following words:

a̸oût	[u] *or* [ut]	*August*
le curaça̸o	[kyraso]	*curaçao (a liqueur)*
la Sa̸ône	[son]	*Saône (river)*
le paøn	[pɑ̃]	*peacock*
le faøn	[fɑ̃]	*fawn*
l'oi̸gnon	[ɔɲɔ̃]	*onion*

Note: The combination **mn** does not indicate the nasalization of the preceding vowel, whereas **nm** does:

automne	[otɔn]
indemniser	[ɛ̃dɛmnize]
somnambule	[sɔmnɑ̃byl]
hymne	[imnə]
calomnie	[kalɔmni]
gymnase	[ʒimnɑz]

But: nous vînmes [vɛ̃m]

EXERCISE

Pronounce:

1. domptable
2. indomptable
3. indemniser
4. exempt
5. exempte
6. le baptême
7. le faon
8. en automne
9. condamner
10. la promptitude
11. la sculpture
12. le sculpteur
13. promptement
14. le comptable
15. le comptoir
16. la comptabilité
17. sculpter
18. baptiser
19. les oignons
20. les paons
21. le compteur
22. le dompteur
23. sculptural
24. la dompteuse
25. condamnable
26. la condamnation
27. l'hymnaire
28. exempté
29. St. Jean-Baptiste
30. le baptistère

CHAPTER XIX

LETTERS PRONOUNCED IRREGULARLY

44

There are a few individual words and one group of words in which a letter stands for a sound different from those that it indicates in its common uses.

44.1 The **a** of ***hall*** is pronounced [o].

44.2 The **d** of ***médecin*** is pronounced [t].

44.3 ***Monsieur*** has the very irregular pronunciation [məsjø].

44.4 The **c** of ***second*** and its derivatives is pronounced [g].

44.5 The **e** followed by **mm** or **nn** in *1)* ***femme,*** *2)* ***solennel*** and its derivatives, *3)* all adverbs ending in **-emment,** is pronounced [a].[1]

EXERCISE

Pronounce:

1. intelligemment
2. évidemment
3. solennel
4. solenniser
5. secondaire
6. secondement
7. seconder
8. patiemment
9. fréquemment
10. prudemment
11. différemment
12. récemment
13. innocemment
14. violemment
15. ardemment
16. apparemment
17. consciemment
18. insolemment
19. indépendemment
20. diligemment

[1] This makes these adverbs, in the sound of their ending, identical with the large group of adverbs which actually do have the letter **a** in the spelling: *élégamment, constamment,* etc.

CHAPTER XX

Diaeresis

45

The **diaeresis** (*tréma*) over the second of two vowels means that it is to be pronounced separately, receiving the sound which is ordinarily given when it is the only vowel in the syllable.

45.1 The **diaeresis** occurs most frequently over the letter **i.** In the following words the **ï** is pronounced [i].

l'archaïsme	l'égoïsme
aïe!	le maïs
haïr	naïf, naïve
inouï [inwi]	Thaïs [tais]
égoïste	

45.2 Between two vowel sounds the **ï** is pronounced [j]. (This illustrates the rule that **i** followed by another vowel becomes the semi-consonant (j): *viens, étudions.*)

le païen [pajɛ̃]
l'aïeul [ajœl]
le glaïeul [glajœl]

45.3 Over the **e** the **diaeresis** would usually indicate that the **ë** is pronounced [ɛ]—for example, *Noël;* but in the ending **-guë,** the significance is that the **u** is to be pronounced (*aiguë* [egy]) rather than treated as a part of the digraph **gu** indicating the hard sound of **g** (*blague* [blag]). See Paragraph 32.

EXERCISE

Pronounce:

1. il hait *he hates*
   il haït *he hated*
2. tu hais
   tu haïs
3. mais
   le maïs
4. le glaive
   naïve
5. froide
   le sphéroïde
6. la bague
   aiguë
7. pair
   haïr
8. que j'aie
   aïe!
9. l'angoisse
   l'égoïsme
10. coincer
    coïncider
11. la guitare
    l'ambiguïté
12. roide
    l'astéroïde
13. le roi
    héroïque
14. républicain
    Caïn
15. que je naisse
    Thaïs
16. l'Oise
    Héloïse
17. la figue
    la ciguë
18. l'aine
    la cocaïne
19. archaïque
20. laïc
21. le stoïcien
22. l'ouïe [wi]
23. prosaïque
24. Noël
25. Israël
26. Isaïe
27. Moïse
28. Mont Sinaï
29. la Jamaïque
30. Hanoï

CHAPTER XXI

Liaison

46

Liaison, the linking of French words by pronouncing an otherwise silent consonant when the next word begins with a vowel sound, can be fully learned only by imitating cultivated French speech. The number of liaisons varies with age groups, degree of culture, speed of delivery, kind of delivery (spontaneous speech or reading), and type of material (prose or poetry). The number of required liaisons tends to diminish in modern French. However, there are certain minimum linkings that all cultivated people make in ordinary speech.

46.1 Between articles and nouns:

les‿amis, les‿hôtels, aux‿hommes, des‿arbres

46.2 Between an adjective and a noun if the adjective comes first:

les gros‿arbres, un petit‿avion

46.3 Between personal pronoun (subject or object) and verb:

ils‿ont, on‿écoute, on les‿écoute, nous‿en‿avons, veut‿-il, vend‿-il

46.4 Between preposition and object, particularly the one-syllable prepositions: ***dans, en, chez, sous, dès.***

sans‿amis, en‿argent, après‿avoir bu

Of the longer prepositions, ***selon*** is never linked.

46.5 Forms of ***être*** and ***avoir*** tend to be linked to the next word.

Il est‿ici. Ils sont‿arrivés.

46.6 Short adverbs are linked with a following adjective, adverb, or past participle. In the case of ***pas, bien,*** and ***très,*** this is practically invariable.

pas‿assez très‿heureux bien‿élevé

46.7 There are a certain number of clichés in which the liaison is traditionally made, although it is outside the above rules.

pas‿à pas
de plus‿en plus
de moins‿en moins
tout‿à coup
tout‿à fait
tout‿à l'heure
Champs‿Élysées
États‿Unis
un fait‿acompli
vis‿à-vis
nuit‿et jour
accent‿aigu

This list includes some of the most common cases. Others become obvious as one is increasingly exposed to spoken French.

47

The **t** of *et* is never pronounced. Be careful also not to make any linking with an **aspirate h.** (See Chapter XVI.) The change of meaning which often results if a liaison is mistakenly made with an **aspirate h** can be seen in the following:

Aspirate h:	*Meaning conveyed by linking:*
les héros	les zéros
les hauteurs	les‿auteurs
les hêtres	les‿êtres

47.1 The linking is so completely excluded in the case of an **aspirate h** that a **mute e** is sounded if necessary to keep a consonant from being carried over from a preceding word:

une hauteur   une bonne hache

48

D final is carried over as [t]; **x** and **s** as [z]; **f** as [v] with *ans, années, heures,* otherwise usually as [f]. (See Paragraph 49.9.)

comprend‿il? [t]	tend‿elle? [t]	rend‿on? [t]
deux‿enfants [z]	six‿éléphants [z]	neuf‿heures [v]

EXERCISE

All the following phrases and sentences contain examples of liaison, with the exception of a few cases where a **mute h** is introduced.

1. ces arbres
2. ces gros arbres
3. un grand avion
4. de grands avions
5. aux étudiants
6. aux autres étudiants
7. aux angles
8. des hameaux (le hameau)
9. de bonnes affaires
10. deux entreprises

11. six erreurs
12. en plein air
13. huit enfants
14. trois universités
15. des herbes
16. mes anciens amis
17. un profond abîme
18. le moyen âge
19. le second empire
20. de jeunes artistes
21. les nobles hommes
22. le grand acteur
23. un excellent artiste
24. les faux amis
25. les hôtels
26. les bons hôtels
27. de grands acteurs
28. un grand arbre
29. après être parti
30. après être allé
31. après avoir ôté
32. après une pareille soirée
33. sans accepter
34. sans autre moyen
35. sans assez de force
36. en entrant
37. en accompagnant
38. sous un arbre
39. sous une autre forme
40. dans un théâtre
41. Ils ont occupé le parc.
42. Vous en avez trop.
43. Avaient-ils faim?
44. Les entendez-vous?
45. Ils en ont appris.
46. C'est un ami.
47. Il est en France.
48. Il est avocat.
49. Il n'est pas avocat.
50. Ils sont endormis.
51. Elles sont très bien habillées.
52. Ces horreurs sont à peine terminées.
53. Elles ont aimé les autres héros.
54. Vous avez évité les hauteurs.
55. Les a-t-on appris?
56. Nous habitons là.
57. Perd-on ses amis?
58. Dort-il?
59. Sert-il des apéritifs?
60. Les vend-elle?
61. Étend-il son habit?
62. Répand-il ses propres idées?
63. Surprend-on nos acteurs?
64. Comprend-elle bien?
65. Rend-on ces exercices?
66. Ils sont très heureux.
67. Paul est bien élevé.
68. Il n'est pas assez fort.
69. Ils ne sont pas alertes.
70. Il est très affecté.
71. Vous êtes bien aimable.
72. L'œuvre n'est pas encore fini.
73. Il est arrivé chez eux.
74. Ces enchaînements se font devant un adjectif.
75. Attend-il depuis une heure?

CHAPTER XXII

Numerals

49

The numerals have so many irregularities of pronunciation that they need to be considered separately. Naturally, some of the principles involved overlap rules of pronunciation treated elsewhere in this manual.

Following is the pronunciation of the numerals when they stand alone. The listing is limited to those whose pronunciation requires some comment.

un, une	[œ̃] [yn]
deux	[dø]
trois	[trwɑ]
quatre	[katr]
cinq	[sɛ̃k]
six	[sis]
sept	[sɛt]
huit	[ɥit]
neuf	[nœf]
dix	[dis]
onze	[ɔ̃z]
douze	[duz]
treize	[trɛz]
quatorze	[katɔrz]
quinze	[kɛ̃z]
seize	[sɛz]
dix-sept	[dissɛt]
dix-huit	[dizɥit]
dix-neuf	[diznœf]
vingt	[vɛ̃]
vingt et un	[vɛ̃teœ̃]
vingt-deux	[vɛ̃tdø]
vingt-trois	[vɛ̃ttrwɑ]
vingt-quatre	[vɛ̃tkatr]
vingt-cinq	[vɛ̃tsɛ̃k]
vingt-six	[vɛ̃tsis]
vingt-sept	[vɛ̃tsɛt]
vingt-huit	[vɛ̃tɥit]
vingt-neuf	[vɛ̃tnœf]
. . . .	
soixante	[swasɑ̃t]
soixante et un	[swasɑ̃teœ̃]
soixante-deux	[swasɑ̃tdø]
etc.	
quatre-vingts	[katrəvɛ̃]
quatre-vingt-un	[katrəvɛ̃œ̃]
quatre-vingt-deux	[katrəvɛ̃dø]
etc.	
cent	[sɑ̃]
cent un	[sɑ̃œ̃]
. . . .	
deux cents	[døsɑ̃]
deux cent un	[døsɑ̃œ̃]

49.1 In ***un*** the **n** nasalizes the **u**, but it is also pronounced in liaison with a following vowel sound. The following examples show the ***un*** before a consonant, a vowel, and a **mute h**:

un tour	un‿art	un‿homme
[œ̃]	[œ̃n]	[œ̃n]

49.2 The **x** of ***deux*** is linked as a **z**, as noted in Paragraph 49.

deux choses	deux‿autres
[dø]	[døz]

49.3 ***Cinq, six, sept, huit, neuf, dix*** always have the final consonant pronounced when used in counting, when they stand alone, or when they stand last in a phrase or sentence—as, for example, in dates or the titles of monarchs.

Il est arrive le *cinq*.	[sɛ̃k]
Combien en avez-vous? —*Six*.	[sis]
Moi, j'en ai *sept*.	[sɛt]
Nous sommes aujourd'hui le *huit*.	[ɥit]
Le roi Alphonse *IX*	[nœf]
Je compte: *8, 9, 10*.	[ɥit, nœf, dis]

49.4 ***Six*** and ***dix*** have three different pronunciations:

(a) [sis] and [dis] when used in counting or when standing last in a sentence or phrase, as in the titles of monarchs.

J'en ai *six*.
Charles *dix*

(b) [si] and [di] when followed by a noun beginning with a consonant:

Il a *six* livres.
Nous voulons *dix* chaises.

(c) [siz] and [diz] when followed by a noun beginning with a vowel:

Il a *six* enfants.
Nous voulons *dix* autres chaises.
Elle part le *six* avril.

49.5 The same principles apply in all the numerals which terminate in ***six*** or ***dix.***

Voici toutes mes chemises. J'en ai *trente-six.*
[trɑ̃tsis].
En l'année dix-huit cent *soixante-dix.*
[swasɑ̃tdis]
Jeannette est partie le *26* mai.
[vɛ̃tsi]
J'ai compté *86* parapluies.
[katrəvɛ̃si]
Mon grand-père a *90* ans.
[katrəvɛ̃diz]

49.6 ***Cinq*** is pronounced [sɛ̃k] when standing alone or last in an expression, in a date, or before a noun beginning with a vowel; it is pronounced [sɛ̃] before a noun beginning with a consonant. (Many French speakers pronounce it [sɛ̃k] in all cases except *cinq cents* [sɛ̃ sɑ̃].)

Donnez-m'en *cinq.*
[sɛ̃k]
Henri *V* d'Angleterre
[sɛ̃k]
Je suis parti le *cinq* février.
[sɛ̃k]

Il a *cinq* enfants.
[sɛ̃k]
Il a *cinq* sœurs.
[sɛ̃]

49.7 ***Sept*** is always pronounced [sɛt]. Note that the **p** is silent (but pronounced in *septembre*).

Il arrive le *sept.*
Charles *VII* n'avait pas d'enfants.
Je vous ai cité *sept* exemples.

49.8 ***Huit*** is pronounced [ɥit] standing alone, when last in an expression, or when followed by a vowel; [ɥi] when followed by a consonant.

Le *8* octobre
[ɥit]
Le jardin a *huit* arbres.
[ɥit]
Henri *VIII* d'Angleterre
[ɥit]

La salle a *huit* fenêtres.
[ɥi]
Elle est née le *huit* mai.
[ɥi]

49.9 ***Neuf*** always sounds its final consonant, but not always in the same way; the final consonant is [f] in all cases, including liaison, except with *ans* and *heures,* when it is linked as [v].

J'ai vu *neuf* voitures. [nœf]	Le *9* avril [nœf]
Le *neuf* mars [nœf]	Il est *neuf* heures. [nœv]

49.10 The final consonants of ***dix-sept, dix-huit,*** and ***dix-neuf*** follow the same rules that govern ***sept, huit, neuf.***

49.11 ***Vingt*** is pronounced [vɛ̃] when standing alone or last in an expression or when followed by a consonant; [vɛ̃t] when followed by a vowel.

Vingt hommes [vɛ̃t]	Le *vingt* mai [vɛ̃]
Le *vingt* avril [vɛ̃t]	*Vingt* livres [vɛ̃]

The **t** of ***vingt*** is pronounced in *21* through *29,* silent in *81* through *99.*

49.12 In ***soixante*** the **x** is pronounced [s].

49.13 The final consonant of ***quatre-vingts, cent, deux cents,*** etc., is linked if the next word is a noun beginning with a vowel or **mute h.** It is not linked with a following numeral.

Quatre-vingts‿enfants [katrəvɛ̃z]	*Deux cents*‿avions [døsɑ̃z]
Quatre-vingt-un livres [katrəvɛ̃œ̃]	*Deux cents* soldats [døsɑ̃]
Cent‿hommes [sɑ̃t]	*Deux cent un* soldats [døsɑ̃œ̃]
Cent chevaux [sɑ̃]	

49.14 ***Huit*** and ***onze*** never take elision or liaison with the preceding word.

Le huit mai
[lə ɥi]

Les huit livres
[le ɥi]

Le chef *des huit* hommes
[de ɥit]

La huitième séance
[la ɥitjɛ̃m]

Le onze janvier
[lə ɔ̃z]

Le onzième élève
[lə ɔ̃zjɛ̃m]

Les onze chaises
[le ɔ̃z]

49.15 ***Second*** is an ordinal numeral which requires comment. The **c** is pronounced [g] in ***second*** and all its derivatives.

Le *second* livre
Le *second* empire
L'école *secondaire*

REVIEW EXERCISES

The following groups of words and phrases illustrate all the rules of pronunciation discussed in this chapter.

(a) un coup
un retour
un autre coup
un essai
un hôtel

(b) deux sœurs
deux honneurs
deux héros
le deux mai
le deux août
le deux avril

(c) trois fils
trois autres fils
le trois janvier
le trois octobre

(d) cinq livres
cinq enfants
J'en ai cinq.
les cinq chemises que je t'ai données
les cinq que tu m'a rendues
Jean V n'a pas régné longtemps.
le cinq septembre
le cinq octobre
le cinq novembre

(e) six étudiants
six questions
six nouvelles maisons
six hommes
Des stylos? J'en ai six.
six carnets
le six mars
le six avril
le six juin
le six août
26 ministres
46 horreurs
66 nuits
86 oiseaux
le pape Paul VI

(f) sept murs
sept efforts
le sept juillet
le sept octobre
le roi Henri VII
27 lycéens
57 variétés
97 auberges

(g) huit assiettes
huit fourchettes
les huit couteaux
le huitième dîner
le huit décembre
le huit avril
le 8 mai
le 18 mai
le 28 octobre
le 28 février
Henri VIII vécut au XVIème siècle.
98 tables
68 autres chaises

(h) Louis IX est Saint Louis.
neuf saisons
Il est neuf heures.
neuf morceaux
neuf acteurs
le neuf août
le 9 novembre
le 9 avril
à dix-neuf heures
neuf nouvelles idées
Le pape Jean XIX n'est pas très connu.
dix-neuf vins
dix-neuf entrepreneurs
79 ans
99 citoyens

(i) dix fois
dix écoles
dix émeutes
dix victoires
le dix février
Louis X fut fils de Philippe IV.
Charles X est mort en 1836.
le dix avril
le dix juin
le dix octobre
70 professeurs
70 images
90 automobiles
90 minutes

(j) le onze novembre
les onze fautes
les onze revues
les premières onze chaises

(k) vingt écrivains
vingt appartements
vingt fois
vingt constructions
le 20 juillet
le 20 avril
le 20 mars
le 20 octobre

(l) quatre-vingts élèves
quatre-vingts tours
80 églises
81 églises
80 hôtels
88 hôtels
80 salles

(m) cent habitations
cent une habitations
cent volumes
cent un volumes
100 nouvelles machines
101 nouvelles machines
l'année 1901

(n) deux cents cages
deux cents animaux
deux cent un animaux
200 compagnies
300 arbres
301 femmes

APPENDIX

KEY TO THE PHONETIC SYMBOLS

VOWELS

[a] A sound halfway between the **a**'s in English *fat* and *father*. The Boston rendition of the vowel in *path* is quite close. Represented in spelling by **a,** by **oi** [wa], and in a few cases by **e** (See Chapter XIX). The spelling **a,** other than in nasal syllables, regularly indicates this sound, with exceptions as noted in the following entry.

[ɑ] The sound of **a** in *father*. Indicated in spelling by **â, a** + **s** or **z;** or in sound: ***pâte, pas, passion, blason, gaz, nation.*** This sound is falling into disuse in conversational French, and all the **a**'s are leveling off as [a].[1]

[e] Approximately the vowel sound in *mate, fail,* but more closed and more tense. The sound in French does not glide off toward an [i], like the English sound, which has to be represented in phonetic symbols as [eⁱ]. The [e] is indicated in spelling by **é, -er** and **-ez; -es** in the monosyllables ***les, mes,*** etc.; and by **ai.** Examples: ***été, parler, parlez, les, parlai.*** (See Chapter VII for **ai, ay.**)

[ɛ] The open sound approximately as in English *pair, belt.* But the French sound is more closed than the English equivalent, and the French [e] and [ɛ] are also nearer to each other in placement than the corresponding English sounds are to each other.

[1] Although almost all dictionaries and textbooks maintain two **a**'s in phonetic transcriptions, there is only the middle **a** [a] in the pronunciation of most French people, as observed by Professor Delattre (Pierre Delattre, *Principes de Phonétique Française* 2nd ed. (Middlebury, Vermont: Middlebury College École Française d'Été, 1951).) This manual does maintain two **a**'s in transcriptions, but the matter is not important because the problems of the English-speaking learner of French do not usually include the **a.**

The [ɛ] is spelled **è, ê, e + two consonants** (See Paragraph 8), **e + a final consonant sound, ei,** and **ay** (See Chapter VII). Examples: ***gèle, fête, presser, sec, laide, payons, beige.***

[ə] The neutral sound represented by the **e** in English *the boy*, but with more rounding of the lips. (See Chapter IV.)

[i] The sound of **i** in English *machine*. Spelled **i** or **y** in French: ***ici, Nancy.***

[ɔ] The vowel sound in English *lost, cloth*. More rounded in French. This is the sound most commonly associated with the spelling **o.** (See Chapter VIII.)

[o] The closed sound similar to the **o** in *hope*, but without the glide toward [u], which makes the English sound [oᵘ]. See Chapter VIII for a complete treatment of the spellings of the open and closed sounds of **o.**

[u] The sound of **ou** in English *routine*, or of **oo** in *boot*, but with more rounding and tenseness. Indicated by the spelling **ou** in French. (See Chapter XVII.)

[y] No English equivalent. It can be achieved by taking the mouth position for [u] and then, while holding that position, pronouncing an [i] instead. Spelled with a **u** in French: ***une, reçu.***

[ø] No equivalent in English. It is usually described as produced by taking the lip position for [o] and the tongue position for [e]. Probably more easily achieved by listening and imitating. It is represented by the spelling **eu, œu,** and occurs as the final or initial sound in a word: ***peu, Europe, nœud.*** It is a closed vowel, of which the open form is described next.

[œ] No equivalent in English. Produced approximately with the lip position for [o] and the tongue position for [ɛ]. Spellings: **eu, œu, ue.** The sound occurs particularly in closed syllables: ***peur, œuvre, accueil.***

[ɑ̃] The nasal form of [ɑ]. Spellings: **am, an, em, en.** (See Chapter VI, Paragraph 16.)

[ɛ̃] The nasal form of [ɛ], but somewhat more open. Spellings: **im, in, aim, ain, eim, ein, ym, yn,** and certain others. This sound is quite similar to the vowel of *can't* as rendered in the American Midwest. (See Chapter VI, Paragraph 21.)

[ɔ̃] A nasalized **o,** with mouth position between the [ɔ] and the [o], but closer to [o]. Spellings: **om, on.** (See Chapter VI, Paragraph 19.)

[œ̃] A nasalized form of [œ]. Spellings: **um, un.** (See Chapter VI, Paragraph 20.)

SEMI-VOWELS

[j] The sound of **y** in *yes*, but in French it is more vigorous. Represented in spelling by **i** before vowels (See Paragraph 45.2), by **y** (See Paragraph 23.4), and by **-il, -ill-, -ille** (See Chapter V). Examples: ***viens, yeux, aille.***

[w] The sound of **w** in English *we*, but in French it is more vigorous, particularly in initial position. It is spelled **ou** preceding another vowel and is also the first of the two sounds represented by **oi.** Examples: ***oui, ouest, soin.*** (See Paragraph 42.)

[ɥ] This is the sound [y] as somewhat altered when it precedes a vowel. It is spelled **u + vowel: *suis, continuer, remua.***

CONSONANTS

[b] The sound of **b** in *bed*. French: ***beau, ruban.***

[d] The sound of **d** in *dog*. Spelled **d** in French also, but pronounced with the tip of the tongue touching the back of the upper teeth. Examples: ***dame, coude.***

[f] The sound of **f** in English *fat*. In French as in English this sound is spelled **f** or **ph: *fort, philosophie.***

[g] The sound of **g** in *go*. This is the sound given in French to **g + a, o, u,** or **a consonant;** to **gu + e, i,** or **y.** (See Chapter XI.)

[k] The sound of **k** in *kid*. Indicated by the spelling **c + a, o, u,** or **a consonant,** by the spelling **qu** (See Chapter X), and in a few cases **ch** (See Paragraph 38).

[l] The sound of **l** in *look*, but in French the tip of the tongue curls up and touches the back of the upper teeth. Spelled **l** in French: ***il, lac.*** Not all **l**'s are pronounced this way; see Chapter V.

[m] The sound of **m** in English *me*. French: ***me, mou.*** For the spelling **m** as a sign of vowel nasalization, see Chapter VI.

[n] The sound of **n** in English *no*, but in French the tip of the tongue touches the back of the upper teeth: ***ne, peine.*** For **n** as a sign of nasalization, see Chapter VI.

[p] The sound of **p** in English *spin*. French: ***parler, grippe.*** In French there is no puff of air following this sound as in English *pin, put*. Usually spelled **p,** but in some cases **b** (See Chapter XIV).

[r] No English equivalent. A gentle scuffing sound in the throat, produced with the tip of the tongue against the lower teeth and the back of the tongue against the rear palate. Spelled **r** or **rr:** ***ri, serre.***

[s] The sound of **s** in English *so*. In French it is represented by initial **s, ss** (See Exercise B under Paragraph 5; also Paragraph 9); **c + e, i,** or **y; ç;** in some cases, by **t** (See Paragraph 34) or by **x** (See Chapter XXII, Paragraphs 49.4 and 49.12).

[t] The sound of **t** in *stop*, but in French the tip of the tongue touches the back of the upper teeth. Spelled in French as **t, th** (See Chapter XII), **d** in liaison (See Chapter XXI).

[v] The sound of **v** in English *vim*. In French usually spelled **v:** ***vous, rive.*** It may be spelled **w** in some foreign words (***wagon***) and **f** in liaison (See Paragraphs 48 and 49.9).

[z] The sound of **z** in English *zeal*. In French it is indicated by **z,** by **intervocalic s** (See Chapter II), by **s** and **x** in liaison (See Paragraphs 48, 49.2, 49.4, and 49.5).

[ʃ] The sound of **sh** in English *show*. Spelled **ch** in French (See Chapter XV).

[ʒ] The sound of **s** in *pleasure*. In French spelled **j**; **g** before **e, i, y** (See Chapter XI). Examples: ***je, rouge, régime, Égypte.***

[ɲ] Like the sound of **ny** in *canyon*, but pronounced as a single consonant sound with the tip of the tongue against the lower teeth. Spelled **gn** in French. (See Chapter IX.)